I Deserve Better

THE REAL AND RAW TRUTH ON RELATIONSHIPS, FRIENDSHIPS, AND ALL CONNECTIONS IN BETWEEN

MAZ DELA CERNA

BALBOA.PRESS

A DIVISION OF HAY HOUSE

Balboa Press books may be ordered through booksellers or by contacting:

Balboa Press
A Division of Hay House
1663 Liberty Drive
Bloomington, IN 47403
www.balboapress.com.au
AU TFN: 1 800 844 925 (Toll Free inside Australia)
AU Local: 0283 107 086 (+61 2 8310 7086 from outside Australia)

Print information available on the last page.

ISBN: 978-1-5043-2256-0 (sc)
ISBN: 978-1-5043-2269-0 (e)

Balboa Press rev. date: 10/12/2020

CONTENTS

INTRODUCTION

I was inspired to write this book because I know how hard it is to be stuck in cycles. With colleagues, friends, family, and especially relationships. The people we surround ourselves with play a massive role in the state of our current environment. I want to help you see things a little more clearly.

The purpose of this book is not to tell you what to do, nor is it to make you leave someone. My intention is to give you insight, clarity, those "Aha" moments, and revelations. This book is written to make you think. My intention is for you to become enlightened and learn a little more about yourself and the ones around you through sharing my mistakes and lessons. I hope that by showing you another perspective, I can help you on your own journey. We all deserve love and we all deserve to be the best version of ourselves.

If you have picked up this book, it means you are ready. It's time for you to get the love you deserve and it's time for you to become who you are meant to be.

Because you deserve better.

PART 1

How to recognize
when it's time to leave

THAT SOUL CONNECTION

Have you ever met someone and instantly felt a strong pull toward them? When you first meet them, there's an undeniable spark and an intense attraction that you both can't deny.

The meeting is somehow like a fairy tale out of a book or romance movie. It was like you both were at the right place at the right time and there was no way you would've met otherwise. This doesn't happen in real life. You think to yourself, *can this actually be real?*

Everything about your meeting seems as if it was divinely guided and orchestrated by a higher power. The synchronicities are more than you have ever seen in your life and it's like the universe is showing you both sign after sign. You both can't help but think you have finally met your match. The one you have both waited for your whole lives. Could this be the one?

As you spend more time together, you realize the chemistry is off the charts and you both have so much in common. You start to open up and share your childhoods, backgrounds, and past experiences. You grow even closer because you can relate to each other. It's like no one else has ever "got you" and understood you as they have. The sex is unreal, and the conversations flow endlessly. It feels like you have found the ultimate lover and best friend all in one person.

Then somewhere along the line, you notice you're both arguing and fighting on what seems like a daily basis. You have stopped seeing your friends and doing the things you love because all your energy is spent breaking up and making up. You're sick of having to repeat yourself and fight about things that aren't even worth a fight. You're no longer happy and everyone around you notices.

No matter how hard you try to be patient and talk to them, it always ends in another argument. You notice your health and wellbeing are being affected and you feel drained all the time. You're exhausted. You start to drift from your loved ones. Your family and friends ask if everything is okay and you tell them you're fine. You tell them you're only tired and it's nothing. But deep down, you don't want to say anything because you're ashamed. Yet the pull toward your partner is so strong you can't understand how such a beautiful union has turned into something so toxic.

The fights are far from mere disagreements. Somehow, they trigger you like you have never experienced, and you see a side of yourself that even you have never seen before. How can someone bring out the worst in you? How are they making you so angry and frustrated all the time? Why is there so much drama? There's no need for this.

As you try to speak to them with honest and patient communication, it seems the changed behavior only lasts for a moment and you are both back in the same cycle, and each time the fights get worse. The arguing gets louder and the reactions are no longer coming from a place of love but anger. No matter how much you try to make it work, it's like you are both stuck on a never-ending hamster wheel spinning into an infinity of fighting.

Deep down, you know you only have two choices; accept this for what it is and accept that this is how your lives are, or get off the spinning hamster wheel and break the cycle. You already know it won't get better; you've tried multiple times. The connection is so intense, and the love is so real, yet how can it be so detrimental to your soul? How did you both get to this point?

Do you stay? Do you leave? Do you try just one more time for the hundredth time? Do you give up on trying to have a healthy relationship and just accept there are issues you both can't resolve? Do you let yourself spiral down into the unhappy or do you cut the ties and end it?

SOUL MATES ARE LESSONS

A lot of people think soulmates are forever but, in my opinion, we meet multiple soulmates in our lifetime. They can come as friends, family members, colleagues, and lovers. Soulmates are the people we have an instant connection with. You know they're different from the rest. Something special sets them apart and you both have a feeling you have known each other forever.

These people have come to teach us something about ourselves. They are usually put on our path to show us something no one else could so we can be redirected onto the right path. Sometimes the lessons are heartbreaking and sometimes they are enlightening. Regardless, once we have learned the lessons needed, we drift away or fall apart from them.

Usually when we meet a romantic soulmate, the ending can be unbearable. It may feel like a heartbreak we have never experienced before and can throw us into a darkness we never thought possible. However, it's through these trying times when we really get tested and lose ourselves, that we start to reevaluate ourselves, our lives, and our path forward and start creating a new life.

Rock bottom teaches us things that no happy moment can. When we are at our wit's end, we want to give up, and we feel we have nothing more to lose, these are the very moments that force us to grow. This is when our real transformation begins. Have you ever noticed looking back, everything that almost broke you actually made you stronger? It's what made you who you are now, and without that setback, you would be on a completely different path and be a completely different person.

EVOLVE OR REPEAT

Life will always test us. There will always be challenges, setbacks, failures, and heartache. If things were always amazing all the time, we would get complacent. No one would grow; no one would challenge themselves to be better. There wouldn't even be such a thing as success and as humans, if everything were perfect, we would take every moment for granted.

The hard times teach us to appreciate the good times. The bad relationships teach us how to appreciate a good one. The trials and tribulations are put on our path to help us grow. We may not see it at the time, but if you look back to everything that has hurt you in the past, does it not now make sense why it had to happen the way it did? Even if at the time we could not see it.

When faced with challenges, especially in relationships, we only ever have two choices. Evolve or repeat. Sometimes you can both evolve together and grow. For this to happen, there needs to be honest, truthful, and compassionate communication. Both parties need to be compassionate and understanding of the other and both parties need to have a mutual want for the relationship to evolve. Once a compromise has been made, action from both parties needs to be made. It's one thing talking about making changes, but doing them is a whole other ball game.

If only one party is committed to self-growth and willing to do their inner work, the relationship cannot flourish. Unless both parties do their own inner work and take the necessary actions toward a healthy relationship, it will only result in one of two things; a repeat of the toxic cycle or the person committed to growth leaving the other behind. How can someone grow if they're being held back?

Sometimes we have to leave others behind because they need to experience their own lessons. Not everyone and everything is meant to last forever. We meet people for a season, a reason, or a lifetime, but behind every person we encounter lies a lesson. We just have to be aware and look deeper. The universe is always guiding us.

SOMETIMES WE NEED TO CLOSE A DOOR AND BREAK OUR OWN HEARTS, BECAUSE THERE IS A BETTER FUTURE WAITING THAT WILL HEAL OUR SOULS.

BUT THEY SAID THEY LOVED ME

Have you ever been in a relationship where the fights were quite dramatic and even borderline crazy? You know those fights that start from something so ridiculous that the yelling, screaming, and bad behavior afterward just didn't warrant it? I know I have.

We had left the local pub and as we started to cross the road, another argument started. My boyfriend was intoxicated. He had gone straight to the pub after work and it was now the early hours of the morning. I really should've known better than to meet up with him. My boyfriend was angry. He was accusing me of being promiscuous because everyone was looking at me in the pub.

I tried to defend myself by reminding him that all the males in the pub were much older than me and could pass for my grandpa. I was loyal to him. I was with him and I was by his side the whole time. He only grew angrier and yelled at me to shut up. I cowered a little and started to speed up my strides so I could get away from him. I knew all too well where this was about to go. He grabbed me by the arm and squeezed it hard. "You are a little whore. You know that?" he muttered through his fury.

I could feel his rage coming on and I started to feel anxious. Everything was shut and no one was around. We lived in a small town and after 1 a.m. everything went dark. "Can you please let go of my arm? You're hurting me babe," I pleaded.

He squeezed harder and yanked me toward him. "Listen here, Maz, you don't tell me what to do, ok? You listen to me," he said behind gritted teeth. Panic set in. I pulled myself away from him and started to run.

My boyfriend was much taller than me so two of my steps were his one. He was also a football player so I have no idea what was going through my mind to think I could outrun him. He caught me as I got to the other side of the street, grabbed me by my hair, and yanked me back toward him. If he wasn't raging before, he was now. He started yelling at me, and as I begged him to stop, he bashed my head on the gutter.

I don't remember too much after that. I do remember I got on a plane the next day and left town only to return to him. This was a cycle that replayed over and over again. Simply different fights, different arguments, different locations, yet always the same scenario. We broke up; he would beg for forgiveness, blame the alcohol, admit to what he did wrong, say he learned his lesson and promise to never do it again; and I would take him back.

I remember calling my girlfriend to get me because he threw all my belongings out in the yard. He was in another rage and was punching holes throughout the house. We lived on an acreage and I was hiding out in the bushes. It was pitch black and I was waiting anxiously in the cold for my girlfriend to drive past so I could run out to her. I remember hiding under the bed with a knife when he came home drunk one afternoon. I remember my friends all telling me to leave and not to listen to his empty promises, yet I always went back. Why? Because he said he loved me.

He always begged for me to come back. He always begged for me to stay in his life. In a way it made me feel wanted. In a twisted way, I felt like no matter what happened or what I did, he still wanted me in his life. Everyone else had left me. This must be love. It is only now I understand that it was because I had abandonment issues.

I grew up without a family and felt like he was the only person who really wanted me in his life. Regardless of how he treated me. I had been sexually assaulted by several men in my younger years and he used this against me. He told me no other man would want me because I was damaged goods. Only he could want me. I believed him. He didn't value me in his life because if he did, he wouldn't have treated me like he did. I didn't value myself either because if I did, I wouldn't have gone back so many times. It was codependency at its finest.

THE FIRST STEP IS THE BIGGEST

I share this story with you to show you that you can come out on the other side. I didn't earn much money. I hadn't finished high school so had no degree, education, or experience behind me to get myself a decent job. I thought if I left him, I would have nowhere to go, nowhere to live, and wouldn't be able to afford to look after myself. I felt stuck. I thought I had no other choice than to be with him because who else would want me and how could I look after myself? I was broke.

The day I finally decided to leave, I took small steps. I will admit he was still in and out of my life for the next year, but I moved to the city, an hour away from him. I got myself a sales job, and even though it was commissions only, it was better than working on the farm. I made new friends from my new job and learned life could be fun without him. There was less drama, no more arguments, and no more tears.

It took me a while to warm to new people. I guess I was damaged but after some time, I learned to see that not everyone was out to get me. Not everyone had bad intentions. I was so used to being secluded in such a small town with the same personalities that I hadn't really come across different types of people. I met people with ambition and open minds, people full of laughter, and people who were genuinely nice with no intention of receiving anything back. I met people who had traveled around the world and saw places I had only dreamed to see. Leaving that town and leaving him opened me up to a whole other world.

LIFE DOESN'T HAVE TO WORK AGAINST US

I actually had to take a second while writing this because I forgot the little girl I once was. A part of me still can't believe I accepted that kind of relationship or behavior. I forgot the pain she went through, the sleepless nights, and the tears she cried. I forgot that I used to want and wish for the things I have and experience now, but back then, I thought it could never happen to me. It took me so long to learn I deserved better. It took me even longer to realize I could get better and it was possible. Only when I made the decision to take that leap of faith into the unknown did my life change.

The universe has a funny way of working out. Only if we allow it to. It doesn't have to work against us, it can work with us. We have the power to create the life we want. It is just up to us to take those steps toward our dreams, even if we don't know which way to go or where those steps may lead. We just need to take that step. When we do, we start to meet people and experience things and circumstances that lead us to where we are supposed to be. We are all connected, and we are the universe. Once we learn this, everything flows a little easier.

YOU ARE NOT THE VICTIM

If we always place blame on the other person, "He/she does this to me, he/she treats me like this, he/she makes me do this," we will never awaken to the reality of the situation. We will never grow nor will we ever change for the better. How can we move forward in life if we place blame on others? If we play victim, we will never take responsibility for our own actions. We can never change another person, but at any given moment, we can change ourselves. It takes two to tango, remember.

Once I stopped blaming my partner for how he treated me, everything changed. I saw things in a totally different light and learned some brutal truths about myself. I realized that even though I was not crying about my past, I was still unhealed from my past trauma. I didn't really love myself. I didn't have faith in myself or my own abilities. I was reliving cycles I had experienced in the past. I was replaying cycles I had seen older family go through and I was playing it safe by not stepping into my true power and hiding behind this relationship. But was I really safe? I also realized that I played a huge role in enabling this kind of behavior by simply accepting it and not leaving.

If you are in a relationship you know is abusive, whether it be emotional, financial, physical, it doesn't matter. If you know deep down, you are always battling with yourself about leaving. I want you to ask yourself, if this is where you are really supposed to be, why is there a voice in your head screaming for you to leave?

If you have children and feel obligated to stay because you want to keep your family together, ask yourself, did my parents show love and respect to each other? Were they good role models growing up? Was their relationship healthy? Once we start to look at our own upbringings, we may also come to see that we as adults now are repeating cycles from what we were accustomed to. Now think of your children and put yourself in their shoes. If they are watching their parents fight like this and see that the other tolerates bad behavior, think how this too can affect them when they become adults.

We repeat cycles even from our childhood. Most are subconscious and many aren't aware they are repeating some kind of trauma, but if we can be aware of this and look to the future, do we really want our children to experience this too? Do we really want this to be how they see relationships? Do we want our children to experience the same things we feel now? How is staying in this relationship really beneficial to the family?

SELF-REFLECTION

It is true that what people say and what people do are a reflection of themselves. We can never take it personally. So, if this is the case, wouldn't it also ring true that what people tolerate and accept is also a reflection of themselves and not the other person? It works both ways, right? They both hold the same intention. If you find yourself feeling stuck in a not so ideal relationship, I want you to take a moment and ask yourself these questions. I will leave these here with you.

> ➤ If I had the perfect partner for me, what would they be like?
> ➤ Does my current partner hold most of these qualities and traits?
> ➤ If I were the perfect partner, what would I be like?
> ➤ Do I hold these traits? Do I show these qualities to my partner?
> ➤ Imagine you as your best self. What would you be doing?
> ➤ Are the choices you are making currently aligned with your best self?
> ➤ Would I want my own child to be treated the way I am being treated?
> ➤ Would I want my child to treat others in this way?
> ➤ If my best friend were in the same boat, what would I be telling them?
> ➤ Does this relationship encourage me to grow or do I feel drained most of the time?

**THE CURRENT STATE OF OUR LIVES REFLECTS
THE CHOICES WE HAVE MADE IN THE PAST.**

➢ I don't know why he gets like this in public. He's totally different when it's just us.

➢ She can come off as being controlling but she really isn't. She just cares so much about me.

➢ I know you can't see it, but I swear he treats me like a queen. The little things he does for me when we're at home, I've never experienced before.

➢ A lot of people seem to take her the wrong way. She's just misunderstood. She really does have a kind heart; you just need to get to know her.

➢ "What is he doing with her? He's so charming and charismatic. He is just the life of the party and she always seems so negative and down."

➢ "She seems so lovely, bubbly and energetic yet he is always so quiet and barely speaks. What does she see in him?"

➢ "Every time I see those two out, she always seems to have a problem with something."

➢ "Why does he not even try to make an effort and to talk to us? He can't even look us in the eye when he speaks, and we are her closest friends!"

In most situations, people on the outside can easily see something wrong in a relationship dynamic. At other times, the only person who sees anything wrong is the one that must go home and be behind closed doors. I can honestly say I have experienced both situations and not one of those relationships were the same. Maybe if they were, perhaps I may have learned my lesson the first time!

No one steps into a relationship saying, "Let's slowly kill this amazing connection and dynamic we have by projecting each other's childhood wounds and past traumas onto each other." If anything, both parties meet, they fall in love, and they have high hopes for their future together.

In some relationships, both can be the "toxic" partner. In others, there's the perpetrator and the enabler or the aggressor and the passivist/aggrieved. Yet overall if you really look at the bigger picture, both are being toxic to each other. It takes two to tango.

Let's talk about the scenarios I mentioned above and delve a little deeper into what may really be going on behind the scenes.

"I don't know why he gets like this in public. He's totally different when it's just us."

"She can come off as being controlling but she really isn't. She just cares so much about me."

Why would someone show their worse side to the public but show their softer, gentle side to their significant other? Wouldn't they want others to also see how well they treat their partner? Perhaps they are masking insecurities by putting on a tough persona for others that says, "I'm the best, I have control, and I know it all."

Maybe they're hiding the fact that they really don't have control and feel helpless themselves.

Maybe it's a self-fulfilling way to allow them to feel like they have some kind of control.

Perhaps deep down they know what kind of person people perceive them to be and they don't want to have their partner think the same, so they shower them with love, attention, and affection to ensure their partner does not leave.

Another question I would like to raise is, what if the aggrieved was also making excuses for the bad behavior of their partner? Maybe they don't want to face reality and the hard, cold fact that they may be looking at their loved one through rose-colored glasses. It's quite confronting to be aware or even admit that the relationship you found yourself in is unhealthy or unstable. Who can be proud of that?

"What is he doing with her? He's so charming and charismatic. He is just the life of the party and she always seems so negative and down."

"Why does he not even try to make an effort and to talk to us? He can't even look us in the eye when he speaks, and we are her closest friends!"

On the other end of the spectrum, sometimes we can see the best side of people and wonder what on earth they are doing with their other half. Our friend or family member may be amazing, loving, outgoing, and friendly and hold all these great qualities so that we just can't comprehend why they are with their chosen partner.

Let's take a moment and look at things from another perspective.

What if our beloved was so controlling that their significant other felt insecure and scared to converse with others in fear that their spouse would start a fight. Then when they went home their spouse might question them on why they spent so much time talking to other people. What if every time they spoke to anyone who wasn't their beloved, they were accused of cheating?

What if our amazing friend/family member was extremely jealous and controlling behind closed doors? What if their partner was so scared to be seen as "too friendly" or scared to be accused of flirting with others that they chose to stay quiet instead? Wouldn't that explain why they can't look us in the eye when they speak to us? Wouldn't that make sense why they go quiet when their spouse is around?

On the other hand, why would someone want to dim their own light and think it's ok to be a lesser version of themselves in order to keep their significant other happy? How confident is this person really? Why can they not stand up for themselves? How do they even think it's ok to be in a relationship like this? Are they insecure?

I raise these questions because these are the same questions I have asked myself over the years. I have found myself in situations just like I have described. I would leave one relationship to find myself in a similar version of the last. Next time around, just a different face, different personality, damn, they even had different names and completely different backgrounds! So how was I repeating the same cycle? How was I attracting the same relationship when I thought I had learned from the last? Was it me?

Now let's look at things from both perspectives and try to get the bigger picture. Who really is to blame here? Who is in the right? The aggressor? The aggrieved? The perpetrator or the pacifist? It's taken me years to come to terms with this realization especially because I am now also calling myself out on my own bullshit.

In my opinion, both parties are both right and wrong. They are right to feel the way they feel but wrong in the way they handled those feelings. All parties in the scenarios I mentioned have the same things in common.

- Insecurity
- Self-Doubt
- Ego

Do you think both parties are showing insecurity? Regardless of how they handled the situation, do you think they were both guilty of worrying about what others thought? "If people knew how angry I got, they would think the worst of me and think I was a monster." "If people knew how I was being treated, they would think less of me." "If people knew just how jealous I got, they would see how insecure I really am." "If people saw the things I put up with, they would think I didn't love myself." "If people knew I got myself in this situation, they would think I failed."

These all highlight the same factors. It shows insecurity and self-doubt. Worrying what others think is solely their egos. What if both parties stepped away and took a moment to reflect on their own behaviors? Instead of blaming or looking at the other, what if they questioned themselves?

"Why do I get jealous when my partner is talking to someone else? What have I experienced in the past that could trigger these emotions? Could it be abandonment issues? Could my father leaving our family play a role in these emotions? Could it be because my mother took off in the middle

15

of the night to get high? Could it be because my ex cheated on me? Or perhaps it's because I was the outsider at school, and I don't like feeling left out? Why do I get so jealous?"

"Am I too afraid to stand up for myself because I saw my mother do the same with my father and every time she spoke up, she would get beaten? Is it because that time in second year I spoke up and everyone teased and ridiculed me? Maybe it was the last relationship that made me scared to speak my opinion because it always escalated into a fight? Is it because I was abused as a child and was scared to speak up then, and have now carried this into my adult life? Why am I lacking self-esteem?"

Maybe if instead of looking at how the other person angers you or how the other person hurts you, what would happen if you took a look at yourself? What triggers you to react this way? What makes you accept this kind of behavior? I honestly feel if we could all look within ourselves instead of outside ourselves, we would come to find we hold more answers and guidance to our problems.

Becoming self-aware is hard. It's a tough pill to swallow when you come to realize that you too played a part. Whether you reacted or were passive. Those who react are reacting from pain and emotions they haven't come to terms with. Maybe they aren't even aware of what triggers them.

Those who accept this type of behavior and can't speak up also need to self-evaluate. What past trauma have they experienced to make them feel afraid to set boundaries? I do feel both parties have some form of insecurity and abandonment issues.

To this day, I am still becoming accustomed to the word *abuse*. For me, every time I hear the word *abuse*, I think of physical abuse. I imagine punches getting thrown, heads getting slammed, necks being choked, and knives being waved. I've learned that a lot of other people think this way too.

Just because someone isn't getting physically hurt doesn't mean there isn't abuse. Abuse can come in multiple forms. It isn't just physical, there can be financial, sexual, psychological, and emotional abuse. Some relationships can hold traits of one form of abuse; others may hold all of them. The most important thing is to be aware and understand what abuse is.

In some cases, even the perpetrator doesn't know they are the abusive one and in other cases, the aggrieved isn't even aware they are in an abusive relationship. This is why it is so important for us to educate ourselves and become more aware so that if we find ourselves in these situations, we can consciously make a change. We can self-analyze, we can reflect, and we can recognize that the relationship we have found ourselves in is in fact toxic.

SIGNS YOU MAY BE IN A TOXIC RELATIONSHIP

- You feel bad. A lot.
- You secretly wish they would leave you so you can just live your life in peace.
- Fights and arguments are a regular thing and you start to expect them.
- You stop doing the things you love because you are uninspired.
- If someone of the opposite sex talks to you, you get uncomfortable as your partner wouldn't like this – even if it was completely innocent.
- You feel drained and tired a lot. The relationship seems like so much hard work.
- You are scared to express your needs because you are scared it will turn into a fight.
- If you do say what you need or set boundaries, you are called crazy, demanding, or are accused of starting a fight.
- Never-ending drama.
- Brings out the worst in you.
- Excessive jealousy.
- You are always hoping they will change.
- They never take responsibility and blame their behavior on you.
- You don't feel yourself around them.
- Your friends and family are concerned.

Take a moment and really review this list. It can sometimes be daunting and certainly confronting but have a think about which points you relate to. If your relationship is bringing more harm than good, it's time to step back and look at yourself. What role do you play? If you were more confident, would you still be in this relationship? Are you just holding out waiting for them to change or do you need to learn to control your own emotions?

I remember being in a relationship after I had been in a physically abusive relationship thinking, *But he never hit me.* He did all these lovely things for me. He cooked for me, he cleaned, he bought me gifts, he was affectionate, and there were a lot of times I felt so loved because I hadn't experienced this kind of treatment before.

When I was on the cusp of leaving that relationship and torn between his kind gestures, affection, sweet compliments, and our mind-blowing sex life, I had found myself defending him to my friends. "But he does all these things for me that no other partner has ever done for me! If anyone were to punch anyone in the face, it would be me punching him!"

Thankfully, my friends weren't afraid to tell me their truth. "Honey we are all married or in committed relationships and all the things you say he does for you, our husbands and boyfriends do for us too! Those are the things your partner should do for you. They are a given! Stop saying he doesn't hit you. That isn't the issue here. You haven't been the same.

You used to light up the room and always had the biggest smile on your face. Now you are always tired, drained, sad and confused and you lack self-confidence. You were the most confident person we knew! Can't you see what is happening? This is abuse. Stop saying he didn't hit you!"

I will admit this was the biggest revelation for me. It was an eye-opener. The words "but he never hit me" were a cop-out. Just because I had been in relationships where there was physical abuse or where holes were punched in the walls, didn't make this relationship I had found myself in ok. Just because I hadn't had a boyfriend who would cook, clean, tell me he loved me on the regular, and run errands for me didn't mean I had found the greatest catch.

I was someone who had a background of neglect. I had been on my own since I was fourteen and experienced rape, trauma, and abandonment through my early development years. Because of this, I didn't even know these nice things he did for me were what everyone else saw as normal and a given in any relationship.

Deep down, I knew this relationship was slowly killing my soul. I lost confidence; I knew I wasn't living within my truth and standing by my morals. I knew deep down that something didn't feel right. Life shouldn't be bickering and fighting nearly every day. Life shouldn't be an emotional roller coaster with all energy spent on making the relationship work.

We should be able to feel safe to grow as individuals, accomplish our dreams, chase our goals and flourish into the best version of ourselves with our loved one by our sides supporting and encouraging us. A healthy relationship has fights, we all have our moments, everyone has off days, but it shouldn't be so draining that we leave no room for self-growth.

We shouldn't feel less than when we are in a relationship. We shouldn't be losing confidence or self-esteem. We should feel safe to be open, honest, vulnerable, and most importantly be our true selves. We should feel secure enough to grow into who we are supposed to be.

At the end of the day, we cannot change someone else. That is up to them and everyone grows at different speeds. The only thing we can change and have control over is ourselves. What matters is how we can look at ourselves and the part we play in this dynamic.

If you are lacking self-love, maybe it's something you need to work on. If you really do love yourself, why are you treating someone like this? Or as the other question lies, why are you accepting this kind of behavior?

**THE ONLY PERSON THAT CAN DETERMINE
OUR WORTH IS OURSELVES.**

FRIEND OR FOE

Over the years, I've had friends come and go. Some are still around; some are a part of my past. I've lived in different countries and resided in different cities but what I know for sure, is the friends who are still around are the friends who have grown with me. At times I've drifted from friends because we were at different stages in life, and years later reconnected because we were back on the same frequency. We attract who we are and the quality of our friendships reflect the relationship we have with ourselves.

Have you ever had a friend you've known for years but you secretly dread having to spend time with? Maybe you just stay in touch to be a "friend" and when they do ask to catch up, your stomach drops. You can't bear to spend too much time with them, listening to their woes, complaints, and drama in their life. You make excuses not to see them or you find a reason you need to leave.

What about the friend you are always helping, doing favors for, and are so loyal to but they always seem to bail when a better offer turns up? Last minute cancellations become the norm, and last-minute invites seem to be the only way you catch up. You start to think they only want to spend time with you when they have nothing else to do. You feel like a choice. You feel like their last resort.

Or what about that friend who always seems to think they are superior to everyone else, can come off as arrogant, and whenever you share your opinion, seems to have a way to one-up you? That friend seems to believe they are "above" everyone else and vocally expresses how they pity everyone else because they aren't as smart, good looking or successful. Their experiences, drama, or opinions are more important or relevant than others. They just seem to know it all.

Do you sometimes look at other people and wonder why they have so many friends they seem super close to? Are there many moments where you wish you had someone to speak to or hang out with but you know all of your friends have better things to do or maybe you just don't feel that close to anyone? It feels uncomfortable for you to randomly call or text and ask to catch up.

Are there times when you feel super lonely and wish you had someone to reach out to and hang out with? Friday nights are a regular routine of Netflix, stuff your face, and chill on your own, and your social life is as dry as the Sahara Desert. The loneliness is numb because this is how your life is and you sometimes wonder what it would be like to have a ton of friends with fun things to do all of the time. How does it feel to actually have a social life?

I can relate to all these situations at different points of my life. I've been on both ends and experienced the giving and receiving end of all situations. Now I can say I have found my happy medium. I'm not going to say I have it perfectly right, but what I will say is that I have found what has worked perfectly for me.

In fact, one of my best friends now became my best friend because I spoke my truth to her and set my boundaries early in the piece. We met through work and bonded through partying. She was great fun and I did really enjoy her company, but after a while, I started to realize I was always the one footing the bill. The moment I noticed this, I started to pay more attention to her actions and mine. I do tend to offer to cover the bill regularly, as I like to give and it's a part of my personality. Although when it is taken for granted and expected, I am not so open to giving.

The next few times we were out, I started to pay more attention when it was time for the bill. I noticed she never even reached for her wallet or offered, and I was left paying. I was tired of feeling taken advantage of and was starting to build resentment as we were both earning the same wage. Every time we caught up, it involved a lot of drinking and a lot of money spent. I knew this wasn't the kind of friendship or dynamic I wanted to invest in anymore.

After some contemplation on the pros and cons of our friendship, I suggested we go for a hike and beach day instead of going out and spending money. I knew I had to tell her my feelings and let her know where I stood. I was also prepared to let go of the friendship if it were to continue this way. I knew I had to deliver my message without placing blame and pointing fingers. I had to come from a place of honesty and share my feelings so I could also leave room for her to share hers. There are always three sides to every story; your side, their side, and the truth, which lies somewhere in between.

When I finally built the courage to speak to her and open up about my feelings, I was quite shocked by her reaction. Instead of getting angry and defensive, she immediately apologized and took full responsibility for how her actions made me feel. She explained how she just moved up to the city and was living paycheck to paycheck. She knew I had come from a higher paying role and didn't even think to consider that I too might be struggling financially.

My friend then went on to tell me how much she valued having me in her life and that she didn't want to lose me as a friend. Nor did she want to make me feel taken for a ride. We agreed we would start doing other things that didn't always involve drinking. After coming to a mutual understanding, I felt a weight lift off my shoulders and grew tremendous respect for her based on how she handled our conversation.

We have never had that same conversation again and have never had the same issues arise. Our friendship has grown even stronger and we have shared many fun experiences together. We both call each other out on things and speak the truth even when the other doesn't want to hear it. At the end of the day, we both know we want whatever is best for each other.

This girl is truly my best friend. Over the years we have watched each other grow in many aspects. Even though we have different paths and goals, we share a bond that is not easy to come by. She is my biggest cheerleader, my friend I can count on when in need, and I have so much fun with her. She is my rock and keeps me in line. This girl tells me the things I don't want to hear but need to hear. If I hadn't worked up the courage to speak to her about my feelings, imagine what could have come of our relationship. Look what I'd be missing out on.

I have many acquaintances, loads of people I have a good relationship with, but a small select group of people I can honestly call friends. You know the people you can really be honest and truly vulnerable with without feeling like you will be judged? That's what I call a true friend.

I've had to learn to be selective and learn how to cultivate the friendships I did really cherish into something more fruitful. It's not every day you meet people you really click with, and when that happens, just like any relationship, it takes work to strengthen and grow. People grow, people change, people have different goals and paths, but if someone is important to you, you need to learn to grow with them. Sometimes, you may find you need to accept that you have grown apart. Not everyone is meant to be forever, but I do know everyone crosses our paths for a reason.

Let's look more into the different scenarios you could be facing in your own friendships.

Let's explore both sides of the situation. The experience of having a toxic friend and the experience of feeling like you don't have any friends.

THE TOXIC FRIEND

Regardless which of these scenarios you relate to, the truth is, all of these scenarios suck. Let's face it, we have all at least once or twice in our life dealt with that energy-sucking friend who always seems to see the negative in life and has so much drama going on. Regardless if you go without seeing them for months, it's the same storyline.

Sometimes we find ourselves with that friend who is forever broke, and you find yourself always paying for every outing and lending them money, quite a lot. They always have some excuse as to why they have no money, and like clockwork, you always come to their rescue.

It's also a horrible feeling when someone you care about always seems to devalue you. They make you feel like they are above you and act as if they are superior to you. You start to feel like you don't want to tell them anything because they will just tell you that you need to suck it up and need to grow up so you're on their level.

You're sick of it. It's emotionally draining. It's exhausting. You find yourself wanting to distance from them because you have absolutely no idea how to tell them how sick and tired you are of their bullshit. You start to avoid them and don't want to say anything because you have no idea how to tell them and you know if you did say something, they would portray you as the villain and you would feel bad for having said anything. So you stay quiet.

Resentment starts to build, and you really start to feel like you can't stand the sight of your friend. Your temperature rises around them, you get anxiety, but somehow you still manage to keep your cool and force a smile. Because why? You're a good friend of course. You can't bear to hurt their feelings and you don't want to say something to upset them.

If you find yourself in this situation, are resonating with every word I am saying, and are nodding your head as you continue to read, these are some questions I would like you to ask yourself.

- ➢ What do you like about your friend?
- ➢ What made you want to be friends with them in the first place?
- ➢ What good qualities does this friend have?
- ➢ If you were in trouble and needed a shoulder, would they be there?
- ➢ Have you shared a lot of good times filled with fun and laughter?
- ➢ Would you feel upset if they weren't in your life?

If you find yourself questioning why they are even your friend, and racking your brain to find the things you like about them, it might be time to reevaluate and decide whether having this relationship in your life is even worth it. As the old saying goes, "We are who we surround ourselves with." If being around this "friend" is draining, exhausting, and you feel down after spending time with them, the real question you need to ask is, why are you still spending time with them? Why are you doing this to yourself?

On the other hand, if you find yourself listing all the reasons you love this person, if you can see good qualities you adore, and if losing them would feel like a loss, the questions I challenge you to ask are; Am I being a good friend by holding these feelings in and building resentment?

Is me keeping quiet doing good to our friendship? Can I have an honest and open conversation with my friend and discuss the problem without it turning into an argument?

FEELING LONELY

Maybe you feel like you wish you could complain about a friend, but in reality, you just don't seem to have many, if any. You never get invited to things, and on the off chance you are out with a group of people, everyone else seems to vibe really well and you still feel like an outsider.

Whenever things go wrong in life, you wish you had a shoulder to cry on and wish you had someone to talk with. Even when you scroll through your list of contacts and your old Facebook messages, you still can't find anyone you feel comfortable to reach out to. You start to question what the hell is wrong with you and why you don't have any friends.

Your weekends are filled with binge watching TV series and mindlessly scrolling on your Instagram feed and your weeks are just all work and hardly any play. Life has somehow become routinely boring. You show up at work with a smile, don't have any issues or conflict with anyone, yet don't have any real feelings of closeness or intimacy with another soul. You crave connection and the closest you get to a connection is a mindless hook up, which then just leaves you feeling lonelier than you did before.

If you can relate to this, I would like you to take a moment and do some soul searching. Ask yourself these questions and get really honest with yourself. It can be really hard to take a look at yourself and admit things you don't want to see but only in your own honesty can you find the answers. I will leave these here with you.

- ➢ What qualities do I have that make me a good friend?
- ➢ Do I show these qualities to others?
- ➢ Why would someone want to be my friend?
- ➢ Do I add value to other people's lives when they meet me?
- ➢ How do I make others feel in my presence? Do I make an impression, or do I hide in the background? Can I be overbearing or am I too quiet?
- ➢ If I were in someone else's shoes and I met myself at that last party, would I have wanted to be friends with me?

WAKE-UP CALL

It's a hard pill to swallow when you realize the friend you've known for years does nothing but drain you. You know deep down you need to let them go and you are better off without them, but all the years of friendship make you feel tied to them. If you were to just drop them, you would feel disloyal.

It's also a hard pill to swallow when you look internally and see that you don't give anyone reasons to want to be your friend. You may mean well, but when you really look at your own actions and behaviors, you can see why you don't have many friends.

If you have a lump in your throat right now because you have come to some realizations that are hard to face, I want to give a huge high five. This may sound strange, but you have now come to a level of self-awareness. Calling your friends out and calling yourself out is hard. We try to avoid it; I know I have.

Whether your toxic friend is draining you or your own behaviors are making it difficult to cultivate friendships, only you can take responsibility for both situations. We can't change other people's behaviors. What people say and what people do are a reflection of them. Always. So, if this is the case, how are you contributing to this situation? What is this saying about you? Remember, it takes two to tango.

DAMAGE CONTROL

We have to remember that people grow at different speeds and grow in different ways. We all have different paths and we all need to learn different lessons. Some people are not meant to stay in our lives forever. If you look back at anyone in your life, whether they are still in your life or not, everyone has served a purpose. If you look closely, everyone has something to teach us. Whether we know it or not. Life is a constant exchange. This is the cycle of humanity. We come to people's lives to give a lesson or learn a lesson. Sometimes it can work both ways, but every time, someone is learning a lesson. Most of the time we are not aware of this. It's something that happens subconsciously.

I'm a big believer in the law of attraction. If you haven't heard of it, I recommend reading the book *The Secret* or looking up famous celebrities and role models who speak of it like Louise Hay, Bob Proctor, Esther Hicks, Oprah, Jim Carrey, Arnold Schwarzenegger, Kanye, and many more. What we think about can manifest and we attract the energy we are.

Have you noticed that when we focus on the negative traits of people, we almost always keep meeting people with similar traits? When we focus on the good traits of people, we seem to see good traits in others we meet too. So let's simplify it. If you say to yourself, "I'm sick of my friends. They're all so obnoxious and I can't stand them," this is the energy you are putting out to the universe, so the universe will respond to you by giving you more people who frustrate you. It will give you more reasons to be frustrated.

Now let's switch this. If you were to think, *I really appreciate my friends. They give me so much value and bring so much happiness to my life in their own individual ways,* I guarantee you will start seeing the beauty in people and start attracting genuine people into your life. On the chance you meet someone with bad intentions, you will know it right away. Then it is your decision to not get involved.

LOOKING INWARD

You may even be thinking, *How is this relevant to my toxic friend or to the reason I have no friends?* I wanted to touch on the Law of Attraction, so you had a better understanding of what I am about to say next.

Let's say you have big dreams, have goals you want to accomplish, or dream of having great, genuine relationships around you. The universe will always bring you challenges, not to break you (even though you may at times feel like you're being tested to your limit), but to strengthen you and teach you lessons along the way.

If you want to level up in life, you need to learn to recognize what is bringing you down. When you are growing, not everything and everyone can come with you. It doesn't need to come from a vindictive or malicious place, it is just part of the cycle of life and what it means to level up. Every next level of life demands a different version of us. Look back at yourself three months ago and even three years ago. Were you the same? How different were your thoughts and actions?

It could be others external of yourself holding you back from the happiness you want, but if you really dig deep, it's never others, it's always us. As I said earlier, what people say and what people do are a reflection of themselves. Always. So, if you have friends in your life you feel are toxic, you need to ask yourself why you haven't spoken up. If you have spoken up and they didn't take any accountability for how they made you feel, then the real question is, why are you still their friend? Why are you doing this to yourself? Is there a part of you that needs healing? Maybe you have abandonment issues or maybe you feel it is being disloyal if you leave. But wouldn't this say you are being disloyal to yourself?

If you know your friend means no harm but is making you feel this way about them, the real question is, why are you taking it so personally? Why are you letting their behaviors get the best of you? What do you need to work on? If you feel your toxic friend is in fact someone you want to keep in your life, I suggest having an open conversation with them. Don't point fingers and start saying, "You do this, you do that, you're horrible, etc."

This will definitely get you nowhere unless your friend is also self-aware and doesn't take your anger spurts personally.

Instead, come from a place of love and say, "When this happens, I feel..." Or "I feel like every time we catch up, it's always last minute. I know you don't mean it in this way, but it makes me feel like I'm last resort and an option. I would love if sometimes we could plan things in advance and book dates in." Come from a place of understanding. If you value the friendship, you won't want to hurt them but your goal is to come to a compromise where you are both aware of each other's feelings. You can set boundaries without pointing fingers and placing blame.

If you feel like your friend talks too much about their own stuff and you wish you had more airtime, there's no need to say, "All you do is talk about yourself. I'm always listening to your stuff, and to be frank, I'm over listening to you." Think about it. If someone you cared about said this to you, wouldn't that make you feel like you couldn't tell this person things anymore?

It would certainly make you not want to be open with them anymore. If this person is someone you value and want in your life, you also need to learn tact and deliver your message without being self-righteous. Again, this is where we need to look at ourselves and admit to the part we play in this dynamic.

I once had a friend write me a letter just after a breakup. The letter was about how she felt I was overpowering in our friendship and felt undervalued by me. She explained how she felt like she was the one always asking me questions and I was the one always talking. She felt like she was my dumping ground to offload but couldn't offload to me.

I won't lie, it wasn't a short letter and I do feel she could've had more tact in delivering her words. I will admit some of it was quite harsh. I won't say it was one of the nicer letters I have received in my time. But at the end of the day, I did genuinely care about her and understood she was just frustrated and needed to get the resentment she was building out. I could appreciate writing me that letter was hard for her to do. Even though at first, I was taken aback by the bluntness of the letter, I respected her for doing so.

She cared about me. If she could take the time to write me a letter explaining her frustrations, it showed she cared about our friendship. She could've just walked away and said enough was enough and given no explanation or even allowed me to share my perspective.

Prior to receiving this letter, I was starting to get worried about her because she wasn't opening up to me like she used to. I would ask her a question to gauge whether I should dig deeper or leave it and a lot of the time, I felt she was super closed off about things and short with her answers. I took it as she didn't want to talk about it, so I didn't want to push. I would then go on and change the topic not thinking too much into it. But to her, me not pushing, not digging deeper, and then switching the topic by talking about something else made her feel like I didn't care that much.

I responded to her letter acknowledging her feelings. I had no idea she felt like that, and there was no way in the world I would want to make my friends feel like that. I was oblivious to how my actions were affecting her. I thanked her for opening up and took a moment to look from her perspective. I could see how I made her feel that way and her feelings were valid.

After acknowledging her feelings, I took responsibility for the part I played. Moving forward from that, I made a conscious effort with her. I will say our friendship hasn't quite been the same since.

WHAT PART DO WE PLAY IN THE DYNAMIC?

Do you open up and say what's on your mind, or do you feel like people need to push and poke to get things out of you? Do you sit back and not say anything? Have you ever thought that people may think it's intrusive to poke at something if it's clear you don't want to be open about it?

How about you open up more and start telling your friend things going on in your life? Start telling them things you want to share and start being more open. If your friend is really a friend, they will be all ears. They may even surprise you by wanting to know more. If they don't, then at least you know where you stand. The point is, we cannot control anyone other than ourselves so let's start to take responsibility for our own actions.

Are you the kind of person who overthinks situations and tends to repeat yourself a lot or talk too much about the current problems in your life? When you are with your friends, is the conversation flowing from both perspectives or can it be one sided? Do you leave room for someone else to speak up and share their own stories? We all know someone who talks way too much. Could that someone be you?

How about next time you are with friends, make a conscious effort to find out about what's really going on in their lives, some people just don't share that easily but deep down want to be able to. Friendships are about give and take and it should be balanced. The moment we take responsibility for our own actions, it makes it easier to understand the other person's perspective.

FEELING ISOLATED

Let's say you are in the other boat and wish you had more friends and always seem to feel left out. Again, you can't blame everyone else. If we always blame others for life's mishaps, we will never grow into who we are supposed to be. Instead we take a backseat and place blame on others.

Let's look into this a little deeper. How do your actions contribute to this reaction from others? Why aren't people trying to be your friend or wanting to spend more time with you? I know I've said this more than a couple of times now, but we cannot control people. What people say and what people do are a direct reflection of themselves. We can only control ourselves. So, if people are not drawn to you, what part do you play in this dynamic?

Instead of feeling sorry for yourself, what would happen if you made changes for the better that only you can control? What if next time you meet someone, you showed more interest in them? What if next time you were with someone, you tried to do something that added more value to their life? Be the friend who offers advice, the friend who makes them laugh, the friend who teaches them something new or be the friend who can be their shoulder to cry on.

If you met someone who offered you these things, wouldn't you want them in your life? So, if tables were turned, isn't it obvious that if you made more of an effort, they too would want you in their life? It all starts with us. Regardless of the situation. We have control of ourselves and if we can accept that we play a part in every circumstance we experience, maybe then we could make our relationships more fulfilling.

BE THE FRIEND THAT YOU WANT IN YOUR LIFE

Be the person you aspire to be. We need to stop blaming others and take responsibility for our own actions and the roles we play. Whether we are the perpetrator or the enabler, it takes two to tango. Always. So instead of wondering why people don't like you or invite you to things, take a moment and look at the things you do. Do you give people a reason to want to be around you? Do you stay quiet on the sidelines? Do you expect people to go out of their way to be your friend? Are you so overbearing that people seem to run from you? If you were someone else meeting yourself, would you want to be your own friend?

If you feel you have a problem with your friend, speak up. Speak from a place of love and understanding instead of pointing blame. If you can be the bigger person and be honest and open and your friend doesn't reciprocate, then you now know you need to walk away. But what if you spoke up and your friend had no idea you felt like that and was hurt to learn, they had hurt you? Doesn't that show you have a good friend who cares and the only thing holding you back was communication? Maybe you were building resentment for nothing. On the other hand, if your friend won't listen to your feelings or point of view . . . that speaks volumes. Why are you staying in this dynamic?

**BE THE FRIEND TO OTHERS AS YOU
WOULD WANT FOR YOURSELF.**

PART 2

One step at a time

PUTTING THINGS INTO PERSPECTIVE

I once had a colleague who seemed to point out everything and anything I did wrong. When I use the word *wrong*, it wasn't wrong to me. In my eyes I was just being me, but she kept highlighting anything I did or said that didn't fit in her box. If I was struggling with something and asked people questions and for help, she would announce to me, in front of everyone, "Maz, how do you not know anything? It's so cute how clueless you are!" If I was having a conversation with someone else sharing a story about my weekend, she was the first to say, "Do you ever stop talking? It's hilarious."

It got to a point where I felt like her comments were demeaning, especially because these comments were always made in front of others. Her statements always ended with, "You're so cute though. It's so funny. I love that about you." I felt like it was a slap in the face then a sweetener to cover up the fact she just put me down in front of everyone. It got to a point where I literally felt so undermined and anxious to be near her. My feelings were then validated when other colleagues came to me noticing how she was with me.

I started distancing myself from her because I hated how I felt around her, yet somehow, she always reached out to me. She was always messaging saying sweet things and in public, belittling me in a way that no one could really call her out on because she had a roundabout way of complimenting me afterward. It started really affecting me and how I went about doing things. My confidence dropped and my performance at work decreased.

After a while, I started to step outside of my feelings and started noticing things about her. She was the loudest person I knew. Everyone knew it. She was super bossy and a lot of people tried to steer clear of her but were friendly to her face. She always got what she wanted mainly because no one else wanted to deal with the drama afterward. A lot of people talked about her behind her back and she was also labeled "mentally unstable" by our colleagues. Of course, no one ever told her this.

Each day I saw her, I would start to notice more and more of what I didn't like about her. I could think of a million reasons she was not a good human and the list only grew longer the more I took notice. Every time she would nitpick at me, I would find myself stewing with anger and frustration.

I wanted to scream at her, "Don't you know what people say about you? Don't you know all the things you do wrong? Can't you see how your intensity scares people off? You only get what you want at work because no one wants to deal with your tantrums!" Instead I would say things in my head and stew over it. It was like poison inside me.

I wasn't the type of person to criticize or insult someone especially in front of others, but at the same time, I was sick of how she was treating me. But then I realized her behavior had nothing to do with me. Why would someone want to make someone else look bad in front of others? Why would someone want to continually point out weaknesses or accusations that make another feel less than?

Once I understood that I couldn't change her and started looking at myself, I started making some revelations. Why was I getting triggered so much? Why were someone else's words affecting me so greatly? Why did I even care? Once I started to dig deep, I saw that I was only getting upset because subconsciously her behavior was reminding me of feelings I had from my childhood.

I remember getting "Star player" of my netball team and qualifying for the regional and district teams only to be told by my parents that I would never be able to get paid for netball and to stop wasting time and do something more realistic and respectable. That statement always ended with, "You're too short anyway. You can never make this a career." It was always said as if it was a joke, but deep down, it really got to me. I was always insecure about being so short, and having my own parents tease me for it only heightened those insecurities.

When I was in second grade, I used to finish all my work well before any of my classmates. I would then distract the other students with chatter. To prevent me from distracting the other students and to also keep my mind active, I was then sent to a tutor and had to do work that the seventh grade was doing. I was well beyond second grade Math or English. I then was placed in a group competing with other schools called "The Tournament of Minds."

I was the youngest in the group but being in this team caused me to be ridiculed as a nerd and labeled a loser. Being ridiculed as an adult with little jabs of humor, especially in the workplace (which is just like school, but for adults), reminded me of being teased and bullied in my primary school years.

Back then, I was too young to understand I was actually just very smart for my age and being bullied wasn't warranted. However, to fit in, I started to play dumb at school. I would pretend I didn't know things when I did. Asked way too many questions to look like I didn't know things and purposely failed tests. Just to fit in. How silly is that?

However, in my adult years, when my colleague gave me smart remarks, I would then also go back to what I knew and start to dim my own light, just so I didn't have to hear the "jokes" and feel those emotions all over again. When she teased me about sharing so many stories with customers, I would then start to talk quietly and just talk about the product. It was boring talk.

I really shouldn't have done this because sharing stories that related to our customers was the very thing that helped me make sales. It was building rapport and it's what worked for me. My performance dropped because instead of standing strong in my own power, I dimmed my light to please another. It's crazy to think how being in a workplace environment as an adult has somehow brought triggers from my childhood. Although, the majority of the time, if we really come to question why we get triggered, it's usually caused by something from our developmental years, and funnily enough, we react in a remarkably similar way. We unknowingly replay cycles.

I actually spent some time with her outside of work and saw that she genuinely was a good person, just insecure as hell. She had a lot of drama in her personal life but managed to hold it together at work. She was driven by money and I think it's what gave her a sense of self-worth because a lot of other things in her life were on rocky ground. I learned she really did have a good heart but just didn't consider how her actions could affect another.

If we look at a different perspective, instead of me taking it personally, maybe if I took the time to get to know her, I would learn she was unknowingly projecting her own insecurities onto me. Maybe if I had made that realisation, I wouldn't have taken a lot of things to heart. Just like in second grade, why would children tease another child for being smart?

LET'S FLIP THE SCRIPT

As I've said numerous times in this book, what people say and what people do are pure reflections of them. Always. Why would someone want to belittle, demean, or embarrass someone especially in front of others?

If you really think about it, doesn't that highlight someone who suffers from self-esteem issues and a lack of confidence and respect? Anyone who was genuinely happy, confident, and had respect for themselves wouldn't put themselves in a position to hurt or undermine others. Happy people don't go around tearing others down. Confident people don't try to strip another's confidence. Just think about that.

When someone is truly in their power, has empathy for themselves, accepts that they too have flaws, and embraces their strengths, they are the type of person who brings others up.

They encourage others to be the best them because they too know what it feels like to be insecure. They know what it feels like to feel lost, unappreciated, and devalued. The ones who have done the work on themselves don't want to hurt another.

We have all at some point had that boss who is always demanding, controlling, belittling, and micromanaging their team. If you really think about it, this has nothing to do with the team but everything to do with that boss and who they are as a person. A good leader sets an example. A good leader helps their team thrive with positivity and encouragement. They know how to bring out the strengths in others in order to make the workplace productive.

It's just like those relationships where one is always questioning and accusing the other of cheating. When in reality nothing is going on. They take every little thing to heart and get upset over things that shouldn't even be an issue. It may feel deflating, tiring, and even downright exhausting when you feel you have to always explain yourself and assure your partner.

The number one thing we need to remember is that what people say and do reflects them. Behaviors like this just highlight someone's own insecurities. Maybe they have been cheated on, maybe they were abandoned by their parents, maybe they lack self-confidence or maybe they think you will leave them because they don't see their own worth.

When we start to realize someone else's behavior has nothing to do with our own value or worth, we can then come from a place of understanding and empathy. Every single one of us is fighting a battle that not everyone knows about. The ones who treat others poorly are the ones who are suffering the most.

WHEN YOU ACCEPT YOURSELF, YOU CAN ACCEPT OTHERS

Let's face it, we all have flaws. We all have traits that make us cringe. We all have done and said things we thought we could never live down and we have all done things we are not even close to being proud of. We are human after all and not one of us is perfect. Every single one of us is full of quirks, mistakes, failures, and stuff ups. I'm sure if you really dig deep, you will find many things that make you imperfect and that is the beauty of us humans. Our imperfections and mistakes are what make us who we are.

On the other hand, I am sure if you really take a second and evaluate yourself, you will find many positive traits about you. You will see how strong and resilient you are because of all the things you have overcome. You will see how much you genuinely care for those around you and you will see just how much goodness is within you. Dig deep and ask yourself what good qualities you hold. I almost guarantee you will find many things you can be proud of.

We are all imperfectly perfect. Once we can recognize this within ourselves and accept who we are, own up to our faults, and take action toward becoming a better version of ourselves, we will then be more accepting of others. The rude and obnoxious people are no longer horrible. We start to have empathy for them and see that they are battling with something internally that they have not yet come to light with.

The people who are moody, uptight, and angry are now people who are obviously struggling with something in their lives and don't know how to deal with their emotions. Our horrible bosses may be going through a divorce or having relationship issues outside of work, the friend who always puts us down is suffering from anxiety and battling depression or the colleague who belittles us is having their own crisis and just doesn't know how to handle the situation. The partner who is always insecure and needy hasn't come to terms with their childhood traumas.

All in all, what these scenarios have in common is the fact that people's behaviors really have nothing to do with us. This is why it's so important to be aware of this and not take things personally. I know it's easier said than done, especially when people can be cruel, hurtful, spiteful, and plain rude. But we need to remember that their actions do not determine who we are or our worth.

TO BE RESPECTED, YOU MUST
FIRST RESPECT YOURSELF.

BATTLE OF THE HEAD AND HEART

I recall being swept off my feet while on a journey of self-growth. I met him overseas, and of all places to have met him, I met him at a waterfall. I remember thinking, *Did I just get gifted with a real-life fairy tale? This just doesn't happen in real life, right?*

I had promised to commit to loving myself more and had been single for five years. I had started sharing my lessons and experiences through blogs, Instagram, and YouTube videos. It was crazy to think I was able to inspire others by sharing my failures, mistakes, and lessons I had learned along the way. When I met him, I thought, *Wow, I manifested you because I have spent so much time healing, learning, and growing. I must be ready.* Everyone says how you find "The One" when you aren't looking, so this must be right. Only I found myself questioning the union months later. After everything I spoke so publicly about, I felt like a fraud.

Have you ever found yourself in a relationship where all your loved ones advise you to leave and yet somehow you still stay? Have you ever had a voice in your head tell you the situation you have found yourself in isn't quite right? Have you ever spent time with someone to only notice that you feel drained and exhausted after being with them? Have you ever kept a friend in your life only because you shared so much history and you thought nothing more than to have them be your friend through babies, marriages, heartbreak, and grandchildren?

I know I have. It's easy to fall into the trap of getting complacent, it's even easier to stay somewhere that feels familiar and comfortable. When we find our minds and hearts battling with each other, it can be a really tough decision. Our hearts may say, "You've been friends with this person for years. You've experienced everything together." If it's your significant other, you may find your heart still holds deep emotion for them.

THE TRUTH OF THE MATTER

If there is physical abuse, there is no compromise in that. Hurting someone physically highlights deeper issues that you cannot work out with your partner. These are many issues that only they can work on. In my experience, forgiving and returning back to them only results in changed behavior that never lasts long. These actions are caused from deep-seated issues that only they can change. This goes back to their childhood, past trauma, and relationships. The majority of the time, people like this don't seek counsel. Instead they seem to repeat cycles even with their future partners.

Don't take it personally. Their behaviors are inexcusable, but they are not a reflection of you or your worth. I myself have been in abusive relationships and blamed their actions on myself. I thought maybe if I didn't say that, maybe if I didn't do that, he wouldn't have done that. The truth of the matter is that we are responsible for our own actions. People are allowed to feel hurt or anger. These are normal human emotions. It's not ok for people to lash out violently or harm another.

An emotionally stable person may still feel anger or hurt for the same reasons, but they won't react as your abusive partner has done. When people act out of anger and put another at risk, this is a big red flag. What people say and what people do are pure reflections of themselves. This kind of behavior highlights an insecure person who has no control of their emotions and this is a recipe for disaster.

If you were in a healthy relationship, the same disagreement could arise, but instead of it turning into an argument, it would turn into a discussion where both parties could speak their perspectives. In a healthy relationship, you would both be able to work out a compromise. Healthy relationships still have disagreements, but the fights aren't dramatic and they sure don't put anyone's safety at risk.

When I was in my teens, even my twenties, I dated guys who had no control of their emotions. Holes would be punched throughout the house, I was constantly pinned to the walls, and there were many moments I feared for my life, only to have my partner beg for my forgiveness and promise changed behavior. He would beg and plead, claiming I was the love of his life and that he could not lose me. Me being me, I would want to see the best in people and end up taking him back. The cycle never changed, and the fights only grew worse.

I know we all want that fairy tale and happily ever after, but if you are experiencing bad behavior, you need to take a step back and start looking at yourself. We can never control someone else, but we can control ourselves. Take a moment and ask yourself these questions.

> ➢ What is it within my own mindset that thinks this is ok?
> ➢ If we have children (or if you have children), how will this affect them? (We need to also look at our own childhoods and remember the experiences that cause trauma to us as adults.) Now think of the children. Do you want to scar them in the way you have been scarred?
> ➢ Is this the kind of relationship I want to be in? Can I be proud of this or do I keep things to myself because I wouldn't want anyone else to know?
> ➢ If my partner can hurt me like this when they are upset, what might happen in the moments they felt uncontrollable anger?
> ➢ If I had the relationship of my dreams, would this be what it looks like?

Now, I will say this again, what people say and what people do are a reflection of themselves.

So if this is the case, let's look at things from another angle. I would like you to take a moment and ask yourself these questions.

> ➢ What have I experienced in the past to warrant that this behavior is ok?
> ➢ Did I watch older family members deal with similar circumstances?
> ➢ Have I experienced neglect or abandonment where I am led to believe that I don't deserve better and no one else will want me?

➢ Does a part of me forgive my partner because they seem to beg and fight for me? They seem so sorry and apologetic; it makes me feel like they are sincere and won't abandon me.

➢ Am I unconsciously replaying a scenario from my past?

Everyone's answers will be different, and everyone has had different experiences. I know for me, when I came to my own self-awareness, I understood I tolerated this kind of behavior because I was abandoned at 14. I was homeless and had to survive on my own. So, when I met someone who seemed to be so sorry for hurting me, didn't want to lose me, and promised me the world, I mistook it for love. I felt they must really care for me because my own family left me and didn't fight for me.

We can only make positive changes and better decisions in our relationships if we look to ourselves. We cannot control someone else's thoughts or actions, but we can be aware of how we are. Being self-aware can be extremely difficult, especially when you find all these faults and flaws that make you cringe. Even now, I myself am cringing sharing these things about myself. But I will say, taking the time to learn and understand yourself will take you a long way.

LOVE BOMBING

Let's play out a scenario. Have you ever met someone where the chemistry was intense? The attraction was deep and you seemed to get along like two peas in a pod? You're intoxicated by them and they shower you with compliments and affection. Or have you ever been around someone you knew was bad for you but because they showed you affection that you haven't received elsewhere, you are always drawn to them? You keep going back to them and can't understand why.

Then somehow, later down the track, it all turns to crap. The compliments are now put-downs, belittling you, and every little thing seems to be a fight. Most of the time these people don't even know they are doing this, but this is what is called the "Love Bombing" stage.

This is where they prime us up and shower us with gifts, compliments, and undying affection, only to turn around and treat us in ways we couldn't have even imagined. We are left wondering what happened to the person we met.

The "Love Bombing" is where you can be primed for what is yet to come. You are made to feel special, made to feel loved, so that if they turned around and did something wrong, you would not want to question them. You would feel a loyalty to them. If the love bombing is done right, it can also lead you to believe that you owe them something. It is what makes you feel drawn to them regardless of what they did because they treated you in ways you had never experienced. It also highlights that you are lacking love elsewhere. Maybe you didn't get love from your parents. Maybe your friendships aren't so tight. When we experience this, it always stems from a lack of love in some aspect of our lives.

AWAKENING

Sometimes we meet people where the connection is so strong, it's so intense, it's so deep, we can't deny it. If you are reading this book, I am going to assume that you are on a path of self-awareness and feeling some type of spiritual awakening. If this is the case, you would understand when I say that every single person we meet in our lives serves a purpose.

People get put on our paths for a reason, a season, or a lifetime. The majority of the time, they have come to teach us something. Life is full of lessons and these lessons cannot be learned with just ourselves. Sometimes it takes meeting someone to learn what we need in order to go toward the path we need to be going down.

If you really take a second and think about it, hasn't every single person you have met taught you something? Whether it be a colleague, friend, family member, acquaintance, or a lover? Everyone that we meet comes to teach us something, and if we are open to it, we can learn something so that we can grow. Life is a constant learning curve that never ends. People come and people go. They teach us what we do or don't want, they teach us about ourselves . . . we just have to listen and observe carefully.

MIND OVER HEART

This is probably the hardest thing you can do, especially when you are still in love with someone. When your head tells you to leave, but the

connection is so deep your heart calls you to stay. What if yc
this connection again? What if you never feel this chemistry
get me so much and I get them. We basically finish each other's sem.
We are meant to be. I just know it!" I know exactly how you are feeling. I
was feeling these exact emotions, conflicts, and fears. Here's some food for
thought I will leave you with. Ask yourself these questions.

> ➢ Am I happy with myself while in this relationship?
> ➢ Does being with this person make me feel stronger and motivate
> me to be someone better?
> ➢ Can I grow spiritually and emotionally with this person?
> ➢ Are we growing together in this union or are we repeating cycles
> from our past?
> ➢ Do I find peace by being with this person or is it more peaceful
> being alone?

It can be hard when you feel such a strong attraction and undeniable
chemistry with someone. But the truth of the matter is, if you find
yourselves fighting all the time with no resolution, arguing over trivial
things with no compromise, and you keep fighting and trying to make
it work, the real question is, what is left without the strong connection?

Is there respect? Is there trust? Can you both talk to each other when one
gets triggered, and can the other be empathetic and understanding or is
it a fight? Is this a relationship you can be proud of, or is this relationship
draining you and making you anxious? Can you grow into the best version
of you with this person or are they hindering your growth?

I left someone I felt an undeniable connection with, something I had
never experienced before. It was one of the hardest things I ever did. My
heart wanted him, but my mind knew better. When I left I knew I had
to prepare for the fact that I may never feel this connection again, but on
the other hand, I knew I couldn't continue feeling how I was feeling while
I was with him.

The funny thing is that the universe will open doors for us when we are
prepared to level up. As soon as I left him, I started earning more money

than I ever earned in my life, started writing this book, and windows of opportunities opened up. Every next level of life requires a different level of us, but we can't take what's holding us back with us. If we want better, we have to do better, and that unfortunately means we sometimes have to let go of people who hold us back.

INSTEAD OF GIVING YOUR ENERGY TO WHAT DRAINS YOU, WHAT WOULD HAPPEN IF YOU GIVE YOUR ENERGY TO WHAT ELEVATES YOU?

WHEN FUTURE YOU AND PRESENT YOU ALIGN

This is only something I started to do in my late 20s and early 30s: imagining my best self. I have found since doing this, I have made better choices in life, love, and even business. Only when I started to become clear about who I wanted to be and what kind of life I wanted to experience did I only start to step into my true power.

Once I got clear on who I wanted to be, the universe started putting people, circumstances, and things into my life that helped guide me to where I wanted to go. I do feel that the universe was always doing this in the background, but once I got a clear vision of the kind of person I wanted to be, things seemed to move faster and I was manifesting my dream life quicker than anticipated.

The Law of Attraction is definitely one of the things I have stumbled onto that has immensely helped me on my own journey and it's there for anyone to benefit from. According to Wikipedia, "The Law of Attraction is the belief that positive or negative thoughts bring positive or negative experiences into a person's life. The belief is based on the ideas that people and their thoughts are made from 'pure energy', and that a process of like energy attracting like energy exists through which a person can improve their health, wealth and relationships." In case you have never heard of the Law of Attraction, here are a few statements from celebrities who also believe in the Law of Attraction.

"Make a choice. Just decide, what is going to be, what you're going to be and how you're going to do it and from that point the universe will just get out of your way."–Will Smith

"As far as I can tell, it's just about letting the universe know what you want and then working towards it while letting go of how it comes to pass."-Jim Carrey

"If you can see it and believe it, it is a lot easier to achieve it."-Oprah Winfrey

"That's how you do it. You've got to vision it first."–Jay Z

"When I was very young I visualized myself being and having what it was I wanted. Mentally I never had any doubts about it."–Arnold Schwarzenegger

Now that you have more of an understanding of what the Law of Attraction is, I want to share the number one thing that has helped me progress in life. That one thing was deciding who I wanted to be and envisioning my best self. Regardless of the current situation or who I was or what I had at the time, I held on to the fact that one day, I would be able to help people all over the world by sharing my own experiences.

In a self-fulfilling way, it made me feel better about the pain and trauma I had experienced. I felt that if I could help others get through the same heartaches and learn from my mistakes, it would make everything I went through all worth it. In my mind, I believed everything I was going through was for the higher good. I had to go through it because I was strong enough to overcome it, and I was one of the lucky ones to be able to come out of the other side to then shine a light for others. To show them it was possible.

When I was a teenager, I would sleep on park benches, cold, uncomfortable, lonely, and ashamed. Somewhere, underneath all the fear, neglect, and anxiety, I clung to the hope that one day I was going to be older and wiser and share my wisdom with others. I was going to help people overcome what I was going through now. I guess in a way, it's what kept me sane. It's what gave me faith. Regardless of the current situation I was in.

Many years later, I came across spirituality and learned about the Law of Attraction. This is when I started to visualize my highest state. I imagined being the best version of me. I imagined living the life I wanted. I imagined being financially secure, traveling the world and helping others who were once stuck in a mindset I once was along the way.

Once I had who I wanted to be clear in my mind, regardless of what came to throw me off my path, who I wanted to be was inevitable. It was going to happen; I have experienced many more setbacks, trauma, and pain since sleeping on the park benches, but it was what gave me the strength to continue plowing on in life and picking myself back up. I just believed everything I went through was serving a higher purpose.

I started to meet people who helped guide me on my path, I started experiencing uncanny circumstances that led me in the right direction. Most of all, I started to notice that everything and everyone put in my path were only leading me to where I wanted to be. Every person served a purpose and every failure and heartbreak served a lesson.

I am not telling you this because I am any more "special" than anyone else. I am sharing this because this is what happens to all of us. We meet people for a season, a reason, or a lifetime, everyone serves a purpose, lesson, or blessing. They teach us and we teach them, all without consciously knowing it. The moment we decide who our best self is, we start to understand that every setback, every failure, every heartache was only put on our paths to lead us to where we are supposed to be.

WHEN A DOOR CLOSES, IT'S REALLY THE UNIVERSE GUIDING US TO WHERE WE ARE SUPPOSED TO BE.

Looking at ourselves, pointing out our flaws, and calling ourselves out is tough. It's not fun, it's cringeworthy, and no one wants to admit their own faults, but I do feel that once we overcome the initial shock, embarrassment, and shame of who we are and what we have done or believed in, only then can we start to really build. That's when the growth really happens.

Here are some questions I would like you to ask yourself. Imagine yourself as the best version of you. Imagine yourself as the person you wish you were. Imagine your future self living the life you want.

➢ What are you doing?
➢ How are you feeling?
➢ Who are the people around you?
➢ How are those people feeling by being around you?
➢ What do you have around you?
➢ What are you doing for those around you?
➢ What would life look like if everything were the way you would want?

Take a good moment and listen to your answers. Ponder your thoughts.

Now, take your focus off what it is you imagine as your dream life.

Let's look into your life in its present state.

➢ Is this relationship serving you for your highest good?
➢ Is the job you are in feeding your soul?
➢ Are the people around you uplifting or are they draining you?
➢ If you were your best self, would you be doing the same things you are now?
➢ If you were your best self, would you be in this relationship?
➢ If you were your best self, would you have these friends in your life?
➢ If your future best self were to travel back in time and speak to you now, what would they say?

Now that you have a clearer vision of who your best self is, do you now have a better understanding of why certain people had to be removed from your life? Do you now see why that relationship didn't work out? Do you see why you lost that job? Do you now see why everything is actually happening in divine timing? Do you see why everything is playing out the way it is supposed to?

Your higher self is always calling you. The universe wants you to show up as your true self. It will move things around to help guide you but ultimately it is always your choice. Do you want to stay stuck or do you want to level up and live in your true power? At the end of the day, we have complete control over ourselves. We can choose how we react, how we see things, and how we move forward.

I think once we understand and know who we are supposed to be, every little thing along the way makes more sense. We can find faith in the fact that the good, the bad, and the ugly are only forcing us to shape and grow into who we are supposed to be. We have the choice to move and flow with it or fight against it.

SELF-ANALYSIS

My intention is not to break up happy homes nor is it to make you walk away from things that have potential to flourish. My intention is for you to recognize when a situation, circumstance, or person is not serving your higher good. I also intend to help you recognize if you are self-sabotaging relationships in your own life. This is not for me to decide; only you have these answers.

Now let's go back to your best self. Let's take a moment and pretend you are currently the best version of you. I will leave these questions here for you.

> ➢ Did I show up in the best way that I possibly could?
> ➢ Would my future best self be proud of me?
> ➢ Was I treated in the way my best self deserved?
> ➢ Would my best self accept this behavior or situation?
> ➢ Would my best self have acted in the same way I had?
> ➢ What would my best self be doing right now in this present situation?

**WHEN YOU ARE TEMPTED TO REACT, TAKE
A MOMENT TO PAUSE. ASK YOURSELF, DO
YOU WANT TO EVOLVE OR REPEAT?**

THE ART OF ACCEPTANCE

Whether you have left or decided to stay, one of the major deciding factors of success is determined by how well you can accept what it is. Once you have made a decision, you need to stick with it because wavering can cost you dearly. There will be the initial push and pull and back and forth in your mind, but it's crucial to your own wellbeing to decide what you want and align your thoughts and actions with whatever it is you have decided.

I've stayed in and I've left different relationships and I hope I can save you some unnecessary drama and heartbreak by sharing my insights. One thing I know for sure is that you have to make up your mind as to what you are going to do and then put your thoughts and effort toward your decision. Being indecisive and in between is only going to cause more hurt to you and the other party.

Let's talk about the two different scenarios that can be played out; leaving or staying in the relationship.

LEAVING THE DYNAMIC

Now that you know this is beyond repair and you will keep replaying cycles that only get worse, it's time to pack up and go. Whether it is a shitty job, unhealthy friendship, or toxic relationship, leaving something familiar and comfortable is going to be hard. Especially if you still have love for it.

You already know that you have done what you could, you've expressed your concerns, and you see that this situation is leading you nowhere but turmoil. You have learned your sanity, self-respect, and self-worth have to come first, and even though your heart still wants it, you also know better than to stay in a situation that needs to end.

The doubts start to creep in, you start to question whether you made the right decision, and you start to wonder if you could've done something better to make it work. All of a sudden you forget the things that made you leave and start to miss all the good things. You start to feel anxiety and have a mini freak-out, "Did I just make a mistake?" "Am I doing the right thing?" You start to second-guess yourself. This is completely normal, and it is bound to happen.

The most important thing is to be firm in your decision and seek help and counsel from those around you. It's not going to be easy and you most certainly don't have to do it on your own.

Even though you may not want to ask anyone for help or you may even think, *Heck, everyone has to go through these things. It's not such a big deal. Why bring someone else into my drama?* If you can ask for help, it will definitely make your transition a hell of a lot easier.

I know in my past, I have tried to do things on my own. I acted to the world like everything was ok and I was fine, but behind closed doors, I was a wreck. I felt if I spoke to anyone, I would just drag them down. I felt if I asked for help, I would be seen as weak. I know now that keeping things in does more damage than good. It's so much healthier for your own peace of mind and in the long run to seek help or guidance.

THINGS YOU CAN DO TO MAKE YOUR TRANSITION EASIER

➢ Spend more time with your family and close friends. Even if it is just one best friend you see at least once a week. Talking to your loved ones will do wonders.

➢ Let your emotions out. If you feel the need to cry, let yourself cry. You will feel lighter and much better getting out your pent-up emotions.

➢ Allow yourself time to grieve. Holding it in only does damage.

➢ Even if you don't feel like it, get moving, go to the gym, or even go for a walk. The endorphins will help elevate your mood.

➢ Write a list of all the reasons you left and look at it every time you feel like going back. This will remind you of why you made your decision and deter you from going back and forth in your mind.

➢ Get back to doing the things you love or start a hobby that you have always wanted to do. Keeping busy will take your focus off the hurt and keep you occupied.

➢ Turn your focus onto cultivating the relationships around you. Just because one relationship failed doesn't mean all the others need to be abandoned. You have so much love to give. Now it's time to give it to those who really matter.

➢ Give back to the community. Do a good deed for someone. Giving makes us feel good and also humbles us when we help those less fortunate.

➢ Get outdoors. Whether it's walking the dog, lying on the beach, or hiking up a mountain, the vitamin D will do wonders for your soul.

➢ Seek a therapist or counselor to discuss your feelings. This shows a willingness to work on yourself and improve your emotional wellbeing and can help your future self.

THOUGHTS THAT WILL KEEP YOU ON TRACK

➢ Know it is okay to be hurting and it's completely fine to be a hot mess.

➢ Instead of beating yourself up over what seems to be a failure, pride yourself on the fact that you were strong enough to leave. Isn't that empowering?

➢ Remind yourself of all the things that frustrated you with them and why it couldn't work.

➢ Realize everyone is on their own path and some people can't come with us if we want to grow and move forward in life.

➢ Take the time to reflect at what you learned about yourself while you were with them.

➢ Understand what triggered you and why it did so you can be self-aware and not repeat the same cycles.

➢ Write a list of your good qualities and put them somewhere you can see daily.

➢ Instead of focusing on all of the things that went wrong, start to train your brain to think of what you can achieve now that you don't have them holding you back.

➤ Think of all the things you can do now that you are free.
➤ Remind yourself of your strength every day. A lot of other people get stuck in this cycle and never leave. You decided to do better and be better. Be proud of that.

DECIDING TO STAY

If you have made the decision to stay because you realized you were the toxic one or the friendship/relationship is too valuable to lose, then you will need to be prepared to put the work in. It's going to take a lot of commitment, effort, and correct action to make this work and you need to be willing to put in the hard yards. I will however say that if you are suffering from abuse, I will make it clear that staying will only be detrimental to your future. Abuse is on another level and changes don't happen overnight. Your safety matters the most.

After doing some self-work and reflection, understand it has been your behaviors affecting your relationship. Of course, it takes two to tango, but you can now see how you played a massive role in the dynamic failing. First of all, I want to say a massive well done. It takes guts and a hell of a lot of courage to own up to your own bullshit. And if you can do this, then there's nothing saying you can't improve.

A lot of the time people aren't aware of their own toxic behaviors and how they can affect others. If you can admit to your toxic tendencies and can understand where they have stemmed from, you're on the way to recovery. It's never too late to be a better person and at any given time we have the choice to become the best version of ourselves. We all make mistakes. We are human after all.

THINGS YOU CAN DO FOR SELF-IMPROVEMENT

➤ If you are codependant, get a hobby. Find something that makes you feel good so you can be happy spending time on your own doing something you enjoy.

> ➢ If you find you can get quite jealous, start working on your self-love and confidence. Once you can feel secure in yourself, you will feel more secure with others. It starts with you.

> ➢ Start working out so you feel better about yourself. Your confidence will increase, and the endorphins are euphoric.

> ➢ Read motivational books or watch inspirational videos so you can work on your confidence. You may even be inspired hearing other people's journeys.

> ➢ Start cultivating healthy relationships with those around you like family, friends, and colleagues. If you can show love to others around you, it will make you feel good about yourself. You won't feel like your only source of happiness is just from your partner or friend.

> ➢ Imagine the kind of person you want to be and start acting like you are already that person. You will be surprised, but if you pretend long enough, eventually you will be that person.

> ➢ Seek a counselor or therapist you can talk to and hash out things with.

> ➢ Give up or cut down on drinking or toxic chemicals. This way you can stay in control and keep accountable for your actions.

> ➢ Do a good deed for someone every day, no matter how small. It will remind you of what you are capable of. Putting a smile on someone's face is priceless.

> ➢ When you feel your old behaviors creep up, learn to recognize them and think before you act or react.

MINDSET HACKS TO KEEP YOU ON TRACK

> ➢ Instead of focusing on all the things that were said or done wrong, think of what you both can achieve in the future now that you are conscious and self-aware.

> ➢ Recognize how your behaviors caused damage to yourself and the relationship and work out solutions on how you can adjust your reactions so they can be constructive instead.

> ➢ Don't beat yourself up over the past. Instead remind yourself how amazing it is that you can own up to yourself, face your demons, and change for the better. Isn't that empowering?

➢ Remind yourself that Rome wasn't built in a day, but you are willing to work toward a healthier and more stable future. If the work is there, the fruits of your labor will come.

➢ Write all of your good qualities down and place it somewhere you can see daily. Sometimes the little reminders help us remember why we are lovable.

➢ List out all of the reasons why you value your relationship and the things you love about them. Next time you feel old behaviors kicking in, remove yourself from the situation and read that list.

➢ Start meditation. Clearing your mind and decluttering our thoughts helps ground us and mellows us out.

➢ Remind yourself daily that you can be whomever you want to be and that you are a good person.

➢ Start self-analyzing, have a think about how you get triggered, then dig deep to find what has caused you to feel triggered and react in the way you used to. Understanding ourselves works wonders. Was it something from your childhood? A past relationship?

➢ Take a look at your significant other. What kind of person do they deserve? Do you want to lose them? Ask yourself if you are willing to be that person for them. This will be your motivator to show up and stand up.

ONCE YOU SEE THAT EVERY MISTAKE WAS IN FACT
A TEACHER, YOU WILL SEE THAT THE UNIVERSE
HAS BEEN WORKING WITH YOU ALL ALONG.

PART 3

You can come out
on the other side

GETTING OUT OF BED IS HARD

The alarm starts ringing and even though you roll over and try to ignore it, it seems to get louder. You hit snooze and pull the blanket over your head. As you close your eyes and try to go back to sleep, your mind starts to run a million miles an hour. You start to think of all the things they said when you last spoke. You think of all the things you should've and could've done differently. Your stomach starts to turn, and you cringe at the thought of the fact that you are lying in bed alone. You can't touch them; you can't roll over to cuddle them; you can't call them to catch up. They're not in your bed anymore. Reality sinks in.

Why couldn't you have just slept forever? Why did you have to open your eyes only to realize your reality? Why does it hurt so bad? Why couldn't things have been different? Why does waking up feel so bad? You think of having to get up, get dressed, and get on with your day. You can't think of anything worse so you start thinking up a million excuses so you can just stay in bed instead. You don't want to face the world. You want to stay in bed. Getting out of bed is hard.

Whether it was a breakup, you and a close friend falling out, or maybe you lost your job, it doesn't matter. Losing someone or something you love is hard. You're going to feel shitty.

It's going to be painful. Regardless if it was your first or fifth time experiencing this, it's still going to suck. Even if you were the one who left knowing it was the right thing to do, it will still hurt. You may question or even get angry at yourself for feeling so beat up and broken. You feel that it was for the best, so why on earth is it hurting so much?

ACCEPT AND ALLOW YOUR GRIEF

Grieving over a loss is completely normal. It doesn't matter which side of the fence you are on, separation hurts. It's going to hurt. Your pain is showing you how much you cared. Your pain is showing you just how human you are. There will be days where you can't function and there will be days where you feel on top of the world knowing this is for the best. This will be a journey, a roller coaster if you must. But the best thing to do is to accept you aren't ok and know it is completely ok to not feel ok.

On the days you find yourself breaking down in tears, let it out. Allow yourself that moment to break down. Tears are a way for our body to release toxins and stress hormones. It can help detoxify the body, and eventually when we feel cried out, the pain seems to dull away. Have you ever noticed that on the days you find yourself releasing pent-up emotions with a good cry, you seem to feel lighter the next day?

So next time you find yourself randomly having a breakdown, get it out. It will help with the healing process. If you try to hold all the emotion in, you will soon find it causes more damage than good. You may experience a time where you find yourself crying every single day, it may be every second day, then eventually the tears won't come as often and one day you will realize you haven't cried in a while and that you don't need to cry anymore.

Accept that your pain is perfectly ok, allow yourself to feel the emotions, then give yourself permission to grieve. The sooner we can accept, allow, and release, the sooner we can start the healing process. Holding it in and holding back our pain will only delay our healing. Do you really want to stay stuck in that pain forever?

WHAT YOU CAN CONTROL

You may not be able to control the pain, hurt, anger, and frustration you may be feeling but what you can control is the way you look at it. Changing the way we look at things can do wonders. It can even change the way we feel about our emotions and the current situation.

Sometimes when I can't seem to get a grip of myself, I like to do a little exercise that you may find useful. You may even find this quite strange at first but just give it a shot.

What have you got to lose?

Next time you are feeling sadness, hurt, or pain, have a cry, let yourself feel. Then once you can breathe again without sobbing uncontrollably, imagine all the pain you are feeling and pull all the feelings toward your heart. Imagine all of your anxiety, frustration, anger, and sadness coming into your heart space. When your heart starts to feel really heavy, grab both hands and bring it to your heart.

Imagine grabbing the ball of pain from your heart and pull it outside of your body. Hold that ball of emotion in front of you. Take a moment and observe it. What does it look like? What color is it? What kind of emotions is this ball made of? After observing a little, hold it in front of your face and blow it away. It may not happen the first time, but after doing this a few times, you should feel lighter. Everything is energy and I find this a useful way to release unwanted energy stored within.

It's easy to get carried away when we are feeling heartbroken. What we focus on grows, whether it is negative or positive. Have you ever noticed that when we feel good, we notice every little good thing and the good just gets better? This is exactly the same for when we are feeling bad. When we focus on the pain, the pain only grows, and it is inevitable that we will only continue to suffer.

Changing the way we look at things can seem nearly impossible, especially when we are at our wits' end. Here are some questions to ask yourself that may help put things into perspective. Be honest with yourself and spend a moment in a quiet place. Sit with your thoughts. After asking yourself these questions, take time to listen and process your answers.

Your higher self will guide you.

- ➢ Was I happy in the relationship?
- ➢ Were my needs being fulfilled?
- ➢ Did I show up in the relationship as my best self?
- ➢ Was this the kind of relationship I could build a happy family from?
- ➢ How did I really feel when I was with them?
- ➢ How did I really make them feel while they were with me?

> ➢ If I was living my best life, doing the things I loved, can I see them being by my side supporting me?
> ➢ Did they support me in becoming my best self?
> ➢ Did I support them in becoming their best self?
> ➢ What have I learned from this?

In life, we can learn so much from everyone who crosses our paths. If we take a second to really look, we will find that every single person we meet can teach us something. Life is filled with lessons and we can learn so much about others, life, and ourselves if we really take the time to look deeper than at what meets the eye.

When we feel any type of negative emotion or want to react, instead of pointing the finger at someone else, why not take a moment to understand what is making us feel that way. What people say and what people do is always a reflection of themselves. When others get frustrated or angry, it shows more about them than it does about us. Just like when we get angry or frustrated, it really highlights something about ourselves rather than the person we feel that emotion toward.

The universe works in mysterious ways but if we really pay attention, we will see how the universe is actually helping us. It will put people, things, and circumstances in front of us to help us on our journey. Life isn't happening to us; it is working for us. Every conversation, every opportunity, every heartbreak, every decision, every setback had to happen to lead you to this very moment. Blessings are often disguised as painful events. It is usually only in our toughest moments that we can really grow. Like a phoenix rises from the ashes, our pain forces us into transformation. Only in our deepest pain, are we forced to find strength we didn't know we had.

Have you ever noticed the things that once broke us are the very things that make us stronger now? They shape us into who we are supposed to be, and when we aren't aware of this, the universe will make things happen, pull people and things out of our life, and push us toward the right path. Have you noticed your strength now is the result of things you once thought would break you?

Life is a constant learning curve. If we want to evolve and grow, the next version of life will demand a different version of us. We can remain stuck or we can let go and have faith that everything, good and bad, is working out to our highest good. Change is hard. It's painful. It sure isn't pretty. But ultimately, everything is always working out in our favor.

Whether we see it or not at the time, we always seem to see why it had to happen the way it did later. This is the same for the situation you are in now. I know it doesn't make sense now but trust that in the future it will. In time you will be grateful that this had to happen, and you will come to see the pain was worth it because what is coming is so much better. Even while you are reading this, I know deep down you know this is right. As much as this is a painful process, you know deep down. You have the answers within. Your intuition is always guiding you.

STRENGTH IS CREATED FROM STRUGGLE. HAVE YOU EVER MET A STRONG PERSON WITH AN EASY PAST?

PUSH AND PULL

I'm not going to lie. If you have come to the realization that the dynamic you are in is toxic and doing you more harm than good, leaving is going to be hard. Even if you know this is the best thing to do for your soul and your mental health.

Your feelings were real. The connection was real. No matter if it was a shitty job, toxic relationship, or draining friendship, you're leaving a connection. You're breaking an attachment and you are stepping outside of your comfort zone. Old habits can die hard, and if you spent a lot of time with something or someone, breaking free is far from easy.

I'm not saying this to deter you. I'm saying this to prepare you because you need to be aware that the road forward may be a struggle at first. It won't be easy, and it can be excruciatingly heartbreaking. The most important thing to keep in mind is to always remember why you left and have faith that once you overcome this period of grieving, you will be okay. Better than okay, as a matter of fact, you will be better than you were before.

Deciding to walk away is hard enough, but I feel that once you actually take the steps to walk away, the doubt creeps in, the anxiety starts, and the reality hits that you have left your comfort zone. They're no longer going to be there, your bed is empty, and when you have news you want to share, you cannot tell them. You realize that you're alone, and you have to start over again.

GETTING OVER THE FIRST HURDLE

It's this stage where a lot of people have a little freak-out and end up going back. Most of the time to repeat the same cycle they had finally broken free from. If you can be prepared and aware that your feelings are completely normal and part of the process, it may make it a little easier to keep pushing forward.

75

Breaking free from someone you shared a close bond with is not going to be an easy process but keeping your eye on the end goal; your freedom, sanity, wellbeing, and mental health, is what you need to focus on during these trying times. No breakup is ever easy, and regardless of how long you were with them, if your feelings were real, it's going to crush you. Even if you were the one who chose to leave.

I myself have struggled within this process and found myself going back. Every time, to find the same thing. They would be so sorry and apologetic, I would return, and they would be so happy I was back. They put their best foot forward and showed their best behavior, and the moment that I felt I could stop holding my breath and started to drop my guard, thinking it was safe, the old patterns crept back in.

The one thing we need to keep in mind is, if the reasons you left were because of behavioral patterns and underlying insecurities, these are the kind of things that cannot be changed overnight. Our behaviors and deep-seated thoughts stem from our childhood, past traumas, and past relationships.

YOU HAVE TOXIC TRAITS TOO

It doesn't even matter if you feel you are self-aware or enlightened. It doesn't matter if you think you have done the work. For a relationship to be healthy and sustainable, both parties need to do the inner work. These patterns are buried in our subconscious minds. Most of the time, we aren't even aware of our toxic patterns.

Every single one of us has been toxic at some point of our lives. We are all human and no one had it perfect. Even those whose parents are still together many decades later still have issues from their childhoods. A real change in behavior doesn't happen overnight.

Sometimes it takes the worst things to shake us up and wake us up. Sometimes it takes losing something or someone we care about to force us to look at ourselves and change. Self-growth and self-development can take years, especially for those who have deep unresolved issues.

Separation can only lead to two things: you will realize what a wreck you are and how you need to change for the better because you will lose someone extremely valuable, or you will realize that after some time apart and some healing has been done, you feel a weight lift off your shoulders and you can finally breathe again. The trick is, if we wait long enough and give ourselves time to heal, time will eventually reveal the answers.

The in-between stage can be tricky to navigate. The push and pull, the back and forth. The moments of would've, could've, and should have. The replaying of scenarios in your head. The wishing you said or did something different. No one likes this kind of anxiety or turmoil. Yet we still do it to ourselves, even if leaving is the best thing for us.

If you find yourself being torn and can't seem to understand why you are so drawn to someone you know is clearly not good for you, it's time to reevaluate and take a look at yourself. Here are some questions to ask yourself that may give you some enlightenment.

Take a moment, really dig deep. I will leave these here with you.

- ➢ Was there a time as a child I felt neglected or ignored?
- ➢ Could I be subconsciously replaying feelings of abandonment from my past?
- ➢ Do I miss the person I was when I was with them or am I just lonely?
- ➢ If I could choose between how I feel now to how I felt in the relationship, which is better?
- ➢ Am I missing how the person made me feel or am I missing the comfort of companionship?
- ➢ What are the pros and cons of being with my significant other?
- ➢ What are the pros and cons of cutting ties?
- ➢ Does this person energize me, or do they drain me?
- ➢ Am I a better person when I am with my significant other?
- ➢ Am I only missing them because I am scared of the unknown?

**CONNECTION WILL EMPOWER YOU. ATTACHMENT
WILL DRAIN YOU. WE MUST LEARN THE DIFFERENCE.**

WHEN ONE DOOR CLOSES

How can we thrive in the world if we are holding on to what burdens us? How can we show up as our best selves if we cling to what doesn't serve our highest good? How are we supposed to fly if we are being weighed down? If we want better in life, we need to be better.

It all starts with us.

Closing out a chapter and turning to a new page is never easy. But if we switch our mentality, turning the page can be the start of a new adventure. It's a blank page and we have the power to write our story. The past has already been written, but we are the authors of our future.

What do you want to write now that you have the pen in your hand?

When we gain the courage to close a door that no longer leads us anywhere, the universe responds in such powerful ways. Shutting that door takes courage, it takes strength, and we are guided only by faith that the unknown we are walking into is much better than what was left behind.

When we make that decision and start taking steps into hope, the universe has a funny way of helping us. It is always speaking to us and nudges us in the right direction. When we listen to these nudges, we are rewarded with divine assistance that cannot be denied.

We begin to meet people who help us along the way, signs and synchronicities start popping up to give us clues, opportunities start rolling in, and unexpected blessings come in all forms.

Have you ever noticed that whenever you left a situation, thing, or person that was holding you back, you felt so much lighter? The weight on your shoulders was lifted and your energy levels increased.

LEVELING UP

Everything is energy, and when we are feeling lighter and less burdened, we start to vibrate at a higher frequency. This in turn allows us to start attracting higher frequency people, things, and situations. We are magnets, like attracts like. When we let go of what burdens us, we are showing the universe that we are ready to level up.

We are subconsciously saying to the universe that we are ready to fly. The universe is always listening, and if you really look closely, it has always been assisting us. It was really just up to us to make that choice and really listen to what it was trying to tell us. At times we can look outside of ourselves hoping something or someone can save us, but in reality, the only one with the power to save us is ourselves.

How can we expect to have more in life if we aren't prepared to do the work? If we want respect, we need to be respectful. If we want success, we need to work like we are successful.

If we want to be smarter, we need to make better choices. If we want real love, we need to give real love back to ourselves and if we want to find happiness, we need to find happiness within.

THE SEARCH FOR HAPPINESS

If we are always looking to find happiness, we will never find it. We will overlook the beauty that surrounds us every day. We will miss the moments that our future selves will look back on and crave to experience again. If we are too busy looking for happiness outside of ourselves, how can we truly experience any given moment that is right in front of us?

Many of us strive for happiness and peace, but in reality, happiness and peace has been there all along. It's a choice. Not a destination. Happiness is found within. No one can make us happy but ourselves. If we are always looking to someone else to fill that void and make us happy, we will always be disappointed. And if we aren't happy with ourselves, how can we honestly think we can make another person happy?

We must learn to recognize our faults, our flaws and our quirks and embrace them. Just like we must learn to see the beauty in ourselves. If we don't learn to see our own value, how can we expect someone else to see our worth? At the end of the day, it always starts with us. We must stop searching for happiness and instead decide to live in happiness.

GAME CHANGER

Walking away from anything harmful to our souls shows self-love. It shows self-respect and it shows that we know our worth. Only good things can come from leaving what no longer serves us. Shutting the door and closing out a cycle only means we are ready for a new beginning. This is where our growth can flourish. This is when we start to level up.

It's easy to get sucked into negative feelings in the aftermath of a breakup. The trick is to not allow ourselves to get stuck there. Acknowledge it, feel it, embrace it, and release it.

After all the tears and sleepless nights, one day you will find that you wake up and suddenly, you are sick and tired of feeling the way you feel. Just like that, you decide, no more.

It's at this very moment that the game changes. It's when we get fed up with wallowing in our sorrows. It's the moment we get tired of our own pity party. It's the moment we see that no one can save us but ourselves. It's when we realize that we are better than this. It's in this moment that the real magic happens. This is where the game changes.

THE ONLY TIME TO LOOK BACK

Pushing forward and moving toward your awaited future cannot happen if we keep reliving and dwelling on what's behind that closed door. We closed it for a reason. The only direction we should be looking is in front of us. If we must look back, it's to look at how far we have come. If we acknowledge all the hurdles and obstacles we overcame to get where we are now, it can bring us a sense of empowerment. It can actually help propel us forward.

Decide what kind of person you want to be and start thinking, acting, speaking, and doing things as if you are already that person. If we do this for long enough, the funny thing is, eventually we become the person we aspired to be. Life is like a movie and we are the directors. We decide who the lead actor is, and we create the storyline. The power has always been in our hands. We just needed to find the courage to start directing and taking charge.

Any struggles we have faced throughout our lives have strengthened us. Instead of feeling sorry for ourselves because certain things happen, why not switch the perspective and focus on how strong we were to overcome the battles life threw at us? Doesn't this perspective feel so much better than wallowing in self-pity? Which do you choose to feel?

AFFIRMATIONS TO STRENGTHEN YOUR SOUL

I find affirmations to be super helpful. The daily use of them can help pull me out of self-pity and self-doubt and leave me feeling energized. You can write your own that make you feel good and empowered. Write them down and put them somewhere you can see regularly.

Read them out loud when you first wake up or read them when you are feeling down. Here are the affirmations that I use. Feel free to use them or as a guide.

I am powerful.
I am proud of all of the things I have overcome.
I am deserving of abundance in all forms.
I am stepping into my true power.
I am grateful for the lessons I have learned because they are helping me toward a greater tomorrow.
The universe is always working in my favor.
I am a beautiful person.
People are inspired by me as I inspire myself.
I love myself and the universe loves me.
I am open to the blessings that have been wanting to come my way.
I let go of any negative thoughts of myself because I know they are not true.
I am a magnet for miracles.
Things are always working out for me.

OMG THERE'S A WHOLE WIDE WORLD OUT THERE

If you can get past the aftermath of the separation, move past the push and pull stage, and break free from what no longer serves you, you will come to a stage where the universe starts opening doors for you. Once you release yourself from the negative cycle, you then allow your healing to take place. It is here when we start to notice little signs, people you haven't spoken to start popping up, invites start coming your way, or you start meeting people who introduce you to new things, outlooks, or perspectives that align you with your higher path.

The synchronicities may seem overwhelming at first and you may even start to question whether you are crazy, but the truth of the matter is that this is the divine speaking to you. The universe is encouraging you, rewarding you, and nudging you. It's telling you that you have done a great job and assuring you that you are on the right path. When we let go of the old, we are making room for the new.

I remember being twenty-three, sitting on a beach in Thailand, toes in the sand, the warmth of the sun on my skin, and the cool breeze in the air. I recall inhaling deeply and then releasing a huge sigh of relief. "Why did it take me so long to leave him? Why did I go back and forth over and over again?" If I had known then what I would be experiencing now, I would've left the first time and never looked back.

I had booked a one-way ticket to Thailand and had just begun an amazing new journey. I had never really traveled before, yet I always had a longing to be able to see the world. Now here I was living out my dream and it was a reality. Here I was sitting on a tropical beach in South East Asia. I was at peace. There were no more arguments, the weight on my shoulders had been lifted and I was free. I was free to be me without criticism or judgment. I was free to do whatever I wanted.

Back then, I had no idea that I wouldn't return home for three years. I had no idea I would end up living in Toronto, Canada, and I had no idea just what adventure I was about to embark on. I always needed the safety net of my friends. I was accustomed to the familiarity and comfort of what I knew. I found making new friends nearly impossible and it took a lot for someone to get me out of my shell. I was extremely guarded back then.

Solo travel forced me out of my comfort zone, it pushed me past my limits. I had to learn to make friends with strangers. I had to learn to trust people I knew nothing about. Solo travel opened me up to a whole other world and taught me so much about myself.

If I had stayed in that relationship, I would have been missing out on so much that life had to offer. I was so caught up in my bubble, my relationship, my dramas, my worries, that I didn't even know there was this big wide world out there full of experiences waiting to be had and opportunities waiting to be grabbed.

AN ALTERNATE LIFE OF ABUNDANCE IS WAITING

We all know those sayings, "There's a fork in the road," or "Stuck at a crossroad." This is how life works. We decide which way we move forward; life presents us with choices and at the end of the day, we create our realities. There is good and bad in everything, a yin and a yang, the light and dark and ups and downs. As humans, we can choose to evolve or repeat.

There is world of abundance out there for every single one of us. The universe always has our backs and it always wants what's best for us. However, we have free will and the life we live in and experience now is based on choices we have made for ourselves. If we look at where we are now in this exact moment, we will see how every choice, every decision, and every action we took led us to where we are right now in this present moment.

If we find ourselves stuck in less than ideal situations or entangled with less than ideal relationships, it only means we still have lessons we need to learn. Everyone we meet is here to teach us something. If we are stuck in a cycle, it's only because we need to learn something in order to break free.

Once we start to really learn the lessons the universe is trying to teach us, life changes drastically. We start to step into our true power and experience the abundance we deserve.

IN ORDER TO GET MORE, WE HAVE TO BE MORE

If we were just given abundance, we wouldn't know how to appreciate it. Just like if we never made mistakes, we would never learn or grow. Abundance comes when we can learn to genuinely love ourselves. It comes when we subconsciously feel we deserve it. The good things start to flow in when we are ready for them. But first we need to remove the blocks and self-limiting beliefs. If we are playing small, how can the universe deliver us something big?

I recall leaving a relationship in my late twenties. We had been friends for seven years beforehand. I never expected the ending to be as brutal as it was. He was the last person on earth I thought would hurt me. Whether we were in a relationship or not, I thought our years of friendship meant something more. I won't get into the details of this breakup in this book (I have shared it on my YouTube channel), but all I know is that if we had never broken up, I wouldn't have experienced twenty more countries. I wouldn't have become a bikini model nor would I have been a sponsored athlete. I wouldn't have started writing blogs or created my two YouTube channels.

Sometimes it takes the biggest fall to propel us into motion. When we hit rock bottom, we are only breaking down the walls of comfort and being shaken into motion for changes, growth, and self-analysis. These moments where we feel loss are the very moments that become life changing. Looking back, every heart break, every setback, and every loss propelled us into change. It forced us to look within and it forced us to change for the better.

THERE ARE NEVER MISTAKES, ONLY LESSONS

If we switch our mentality from feeling broken and helpless and start thinking instead that we are healing and growing, how quickly does this shift our emotional state? As the Law of Attraction states, what we focus

85

on grows, so why would we choose to focus on the hurt? Wouldn't that only spiral us into depression?

If we can shift our thoughts to find the lessons instead, we will come to see there were never any mistakes. Whatever happened only had to happen because it had to teach us something that no happy moment could. We build strength from weakness and behind every success there were failures.

With every toxic relationship, friend, job, or situation I have ever left, I can honestly say that I have no regrets. At the time, it was devastating but every time I walked away from something that didn't serve my highest good, only good things came afterward. I met people more aligned with my path and had job opportunities arise that wouldn't have come to fruition if I had stayed where I was. Stuck.

OPENING NEW DOORS

When we shut the door to the past, we are showing the universe we are ready to open the door to possibilities. Letting go of what holds us down only allows us to ascend higher, it allows us to fly. Walking away and opening the door to the unknown is scary. We don't know what will happen or what is to come. We are only guided by the faith that there has to be something better than feeling stuck, feeling anxious and in turmoil. Have you ever let go of something you knew was bad for you only to regret it later?

They say that time heals all wounds. I know it sounds cliché, but it wouldn't be such a famous saying if it didn't ring true. Healing is a process. It doesn't happen overnight, but if we can stay strong, stick to our truth, and have faith in new beginnings, only good will ever come out of it. If we can break cycles that have been deeply ingrained into our DNA, we are stating that we are ready to level up.

Think of the last time you left something that didn't make you feel good. Are you sorry you left, or do you feel you did the right thing? We cannot forget the lessons we have already learned. If we do, the lessons will only keep repeating in our lives through different people, situations, and circumstances. We will keep replaying the cycle until we learn the lessons needed.

Every time we build the courage to open a new door, we open ourselves to a higher level of consciousness and in turn, a higher level of abundance. We cannot predict the future but if we can learn to have faith that the universe always has our backs and is working with us, it may help lessen the fear of walking into the unknown.

If we want to have a healthy, loving relationship, we need to stop giving our energy to those who we know deep down don't serve our highest good. If we want to have happy and fulfilling friendships, we need to stop hanging out with people who make us feel less than. If we want a job that feeds our souls, we need to break free from the comfort of a familiar paycheck and start chasing our dreams.

At the end of the day, if we want more out of life, it is there. It's waiting patiently for us, in an alternate universe. We just need to step away from the dark path we are walking on and start walking towards where our soul is calling us. Shut that door and gain the courage to open the new door. You're at the fork in the road. Do you turn left, or do you turn right? I'm not going to tell you what to do, purely because you already know.

Your future self is calling you. You have felt it all along. It has been speaking to you your whole life. Abundance is there for you and you can really have everything you want and deserve. It's just up to you whether you are willing to take that leap of faith and start heading toward the life you are supposed to be living.

AFTERWORD

As I sit here excited for my book to be released to the world, my heart is filled with so much gratitude. I feel honoured to have been able to share my journey, my lessons, and my truth with you. This book was written while I was going through a breakup. It was by far the hardest breakup I had ever experienced. As painful as it was to leave, leaving him and standing true to my soul propelled me into my life purpose. Walking away from what no longer served me meant I was walking into my true power. It showed the universe I was ready to be who I was born to be.

I came to see that I had broken generational patterns and toxic cycles I myself had been repeating. This in turn triggered a profound spiritual awakening. I had called upon my guides and angels to help heal me. They led me to finding my mentor, best-selling inspirational author, Shannon Kaiser.

I asked my guides to write through me and help me spread a message that others needed to hear and would benefit from. Surprisingly, the book was written over several nights within a month. Divine timing was at play and the message was now ready to be delivered. I have found this process so healing, and I'm amazed at how much it has even helped me.

As I read over the words that I had channelled from the divine, it has brought me to tears, made me cringe and also allowed me to realise the part I too played in my own relationships.

I truly hope that this book has helped you as it has helped me. We really do have power over our lives. We have had it all along. I write this book to inspire you to be able to step into your own power. Life doesn't need to happen to us, it can happen for us. We just needed to learn that we deserve better.

ACKNOWLEDGMENTS

I would like to thank my best friend Samantha Williams for her support throughout my journey. Thank you for creating the subtitle and I deeply appreciate how supportive you are. Thanks for being such an amazing friend and helping me heal so I could step up and shine.

I also want to thank my mentor Shannon Kaiser for the clarity, love, and knowledge she has shared. From the moment I had my first meeting with her, I knew I had found the right mentor for me. The book was written in no time and with so much ease. I have learned so much from you and am so blessed to have had your guidance while I made this book a reality.

Another massive thank you goes out to my brother Richard Peachey. Thanks for listening to me, especially when I needed a shoulder and also for providing feedback and bouncing ideas with me. I am so thankful for you in my life.

Thank you to my old friend Tess Morrison, coming to my rescue on several occasions and for being my rock and sanity while I was going through a difficult relationship. You really did save my life. I am grateful for Brianne B for editing my book and the lovely words of encouragement along the way. You really did put a smile on my face when you told me your thoughts after reading my book. It meant so much to me. I am grateful for the team at Balboa for helping me publish this book.

Lastly, I want to thank all of my family and friends that have supported me along my journey.

Your support means the world to me.

WORK WITH THE AUTHOR

My passion is to help people break destructive cycles that they have found themselves in, turn their hurt into happy and their pain into purpose.

WHO I CAN HELP

*Those who have overcome their own struggles and now want to help others do the same, but are unsure how to start, how to monetize or maybe have started but are struggling to turn it into a real business.

*Those who are stuck in toxic cycles and keep replaying the same experiences from one relationship to the next and are now ready to finally break this destructive cycle and live their lives in empowerment.

*Those who just want to be able to start living a life with more abundance, happiness and want to be able to learn how to remove blocks and limitations so that they can start manifesting and living the life they desire.

To learn more visit www.mazdelacerna.com

Connect with me on social media
https://www.instagram.com/lilmissmaz/
https://www.facebook.com/MazDelaCerna

Find me on YouTube

Personal development, Spirituality and Law of Attraction: Phoenix Rising Collective

Fitness and Travel: Maz Dela Cerna

Lightning Source UK Ltd.
Milton Keynes UK
UKHW011912111121
393812UK00002B/395